THE UNITED NATIONS
A Short Political Guide

OTHER WORKS BY SYDNEY D. BAILEY

BOOKS

The Secretariat of the United Nations: 1962 London: Stevens; New
  York: Carnegie Endowment for International Peace.
The General Assembly of the United Nations: 1960 London: Stevens;
  New York: Praeger.
British Parliamentary Democracy: 2nd Edition, 1962. London:
  Harrap; Boston: Houghton Mifflin.
Naissance de Nouvelles Démocraties: 1953 Paris: Armand Colin.
Parliamentary Government in Southern Asia: 1953 London: Hansard
  Society; New York: Institute of Pacific Relations.
Ceylon: 1952 London: Hutchinson.

PAMPHLETS

United Europe: 2nd edition, 1948 London: National News-Letter.
The Palace of Westminster: 1949 London: Hansard Society.
Constitutions of British Colonies: 1950 London: Hansard Society.
The Korean Crisis: 1950 London: National Peace Council.
Lords and Commons: 1951 London: H.M. Stationery Office.
Parliamentary Government: 2nd edition, 1958 London: British
  Council.
The Troika and the Future of the UN: 1962 New York: Carnegie
  Endowment for International Peace.

EDITOR OF

Aspects of American Government: 1950 London: Hansard Society.
Parliamentary Government in the Commonwealth: 1951 London:
  Hansard Society; New York: Philosophical Library.
The British Party System: 2nd edition, 1953 London: Hansard Society;
  New York: Praeger.
Problems of Parliamentary Government in Colonies: 1953 London:
  Hansard Society.
The Future of the House of Lords: 1954 London: Hansard Society;
  New York: Praeger.

SYDNEY D. BAILEY

The United Nations

A Short Political Guide

FREDERICK A. PRAEGER, *Publisher*

New York · London

FREDERICK A. PRAEGER, PUBLISHER
64 UNIVERSITY PLACE, NEW YORK 3, N.Y., U.S.A.
49 GREAT ORMOND STREET, LONDON W. C. 1, ENGLAND

Published in the United States of America in 1963
by Frederick A. Praeger, Inc., Publisher

Printed in the United States of America

CONTENTS

25125

TABLES

ACKNOWLEDGMENTS

MANY people have helped me, directly or indirectly, to write this book. Although I alone am responsible for the text, I am greatly indebted to those who read all or parts of the book in draft and suggested improvements. In particular, the Hon. Alastair Buchan made helpful suggestions regarding chapter 5, Sir Hugh Foot regarding chapter 6, and James M. Read and J. Duncan Wood regarding chapter 7. To them, to members of the United Nations Secretariat, and to others whose names I may not mention, I record my gratitude.

Special thanks are also due to Patricia Rambach, of the Carnegie Endowment for International Peace, who was unfailingly helpful in procuring official documentation and in other ways. The director and staff of the United Nations Information Centre in London extended every courtesy.

S. D. B.

January 1963

CHAPTER I

PURPOSE

MEN have traditionally thought of anarchy and despotism as opposites, and have usually feared them equally. A system of law and justice is a bulwark against both, and the inadequacy of the legal system governing the relations among states is one reason why life for man is so hazardous. We expect our government to look after the interests of our nation, and are astonished how often other governments fail to understand this.

It is no longer fashionable to glorify war, but to say that war is hell is merely to strike an attitude. War as an instrument of national policy will disappear when nations no longer quarrel, or when they use means other than war to resolve their differences. War is one method by which states seek to coerce other states, or to resist being coerced.

Coercion in support of law is generally accepted within national societies. Law-breaking is restrained by three kinds of force: the force of personal conscience, the force of public opinion, and the force of the police. Breaches of law are punished through an impartially administered system of justice. Provocation, however intense, does not authorise the citizen to take the law into his own hands; it is no defence to a charge of murder to say that the victim was odious.

International coercion in support of law is both more difficult and more dangerous than coercion in support of law within national societies. It is more difficult because international law is relatively undeveloped, and nations do not feel the same obligation to observe what international law there is as citizens generally feel regarding the law of their own nation. It is more dangerous because any war would be potentially

11

an all-out war. An all-out war with modern weapons would be too indiscriminate to serve as an instrument of justice.

There have, broadly speaking, been two approaches in the attempt to abolish war as a means of settling international disputes. Some people have considered war to be an outward manifestation of inward human wickedness which would be abolished if men would only become more enlightened or more moral. They have therefore laid special stress on personal conduct and the power of example. A few have adopted a wholly pacifist position and have refused to participate in war or its preparation.

Others have regarded war as a social institution which could be eliminated in the present state of human imperfection by improving the methods and institutions for avoiding or resolving international disputes, by encouraging alternatives to the arbitrary exercise of violence. Civilised men do not now practise cannibalism or slavery, although the heart of man is no less wicked than it was; unless men similarly abolish war, it is argued, war will abolish men.

We do not know for certain whether war will be finally abolished because men have become more moral, or because they have invented social and political techniques for its avoidance, or even because they are afraid to use the horrendous weapons which they have created. William Penn, the Anglo-American Quaker who was a pioneer of the idea of an international peace-keeping organisation, insisted that "though good laws do well, good men do better".

The purpose of an international peace-keeping organisation is to establish a system of international relations in which armed force is not used, except in the common interest. This means that states must at all times refrain from the threat or use of force against the territorial integrity or political independence of other states. Needless to say, this is a far-reaching obligation, for it means that if peaceful remedies fail, a state may have to tolerate gross injustice rather than exercise force in pursuit of the national interest. When the Nazi leaders were charged in the Nuremberg trials with having resorted to aggressive war, it was no defence to say that Germany had grievances.

The founding fathers of the United Nations established a twofold system for peace. On the one hand, states wishing to join the Organisation were to commit themselves formally to high standards of international conduct. The United Nations Charter includes the following principles, which member-states must explicitly accept:

—Fulfilment of all obligations in good faith;
—Peaceful settlement of all international disputes;
—Force not to be used or even threatened, save in the common interest.

But the founders, being realists, provided also machinery for dealing with the situations which would arise if states failed to honour their legal obligations. It was intended that the collective strength of all should be used to deter or punish aggression. National armed forces were to be reduced, and the Security Council was to have at its disposal military units for resisting aggression. The Charter made no specific provision for dealing with any aggression committed by one of the five great powers, when the Security Council would probably be paralysed by the veto, except to state that there is an inherent right of self-defence against armed attack if the Security Council has not taken measures to deal with the situation.

International equivalents of national political institutions were devised: a court to exercise judicial functions; policy-making organs, consisting of governments, to have deliberative or executive powers; a secretariat, composed of international civil servants, to implement the decisions of the policy-making bodies. These international institutions could together be regarded as the embryo of a world government.

It is fashionable nowadays to regard the League of Nations as having been a failure. The Russians often refer to it as the "notorious" League of Nations, and certainly it was tragic that the Covenant was ignored when aggression occurred. Moreover, the League was never a universal organisation. The United States never joined; Germany, Italy, Japan, Spain, and thirteen other states withdrew from membership; Albania was annexed by Italy, Austria by Germany; the Soviet Union was expelled. Even those states which maintained their member-ship to the end had abandoned the main principles for which the League purported to stand. But the allied statesmen who gathered in San Francisco in 1945 paid a tribute to the ideals of the League when they created a successor organisation with the same purposes and a similar structure.

The United Nations was born, just before the beginning of the nuclear age, in the hope that the unity which had won the war could also win the peace. States choosing to join the Organisation have to declare their willingness to fulfil in good faith all the obligations of the Charter, and these obligations prevail over other obligations. Each member-state undertakes to accept and carry out the decisions of the Security Council and to comply with the decision of the International Court of Justice in any case to which it is a party.

Six "principal organs" were established: a General Assembly, three Councils, an International Court, and a Secretariat. The General Assembly, consisting of all member-states, has advisory powers in most political matters, has exclusive responsibility for the finances of the Organisation and the election of members of three Councils, and acts jointly with the Security Council regarding membership in the United Nations, the appointment of the Secretary-General, the election of the judges of the World Court, and amendments to the Charter. The three Councils, each consisting of a limited number of member-states, are responsible respectively for international peace and security, economic and social affairs, and territories placed under the trusteeship system. The International Court of Justice, a body of independent judges, is the Organisation's principal judicial organ. The international Secretariat, headed by a Secretary-General, must be independent of governments and responsible only to the Organisation.

Related to the United Nations are a number of inter-governmental agencies concerned with economic and social co-operation. These specialised agencies—as they are called—are now twelve in number. They have their own constitutions and budgets, and are in other ways autonomous. The international agency for developing the peaceful uses of atomic energy is similar to a specialised agency. GATT, the General Agreement on Tariffs and Trade, is not strictly a specialised agency but could become one if an appropriate organisation were created to administer the Agreement. Finally, there are five UN programmes financed outside the regular budget of the United Nations, two for helping refugees and three for providing economic and social assistance.

TABLE I

INTERNATIONAL BODIES ESTABLISHED BY OR RELATED TO THE UNITED NATIONS

Agency	Abbreviation	Status	Headquarters
Food and Agriculture Organisation	FAO	specialised agency	Rome
General Agreement on Tariffs and Trade	GATT	international commercial treaty	Geneva
International Atomic Energy Agency	IAEA	related to the UN	Vienna
International Bank for Reconstruction and Development	Bank	specialised agency	Washington
International Civil Aviation Organisation	ICAO	specialised agency	Montreal
International Development Association	IDA	affiliate of the International Bank for Reconstruction and Development	Washington
International Finance Corporation	IFC	specialised agency	Washington
International Labour Organisation	ILO	specialised agency	Geneva
Inter-Governmental Maritime Consultative Organisation	IMCO	specialised agency	London
International Monetary Fund	Fund	specialised agency	Washington
International Telecommunication Union	ITU	specialised agency	Geneva
Special Fund	—	established by General Assembly	New York
Technical Assistance Board	TAB	co-ordinating body	New York
UN Children's Fund	UNICEF	established by General Assembly	New York
UN Educational, Scientific and Cultural Organisation	UNESCO	specialised agency	Paris
UN High Commissioner for Refugees	UNHCR	established by General Assembly	Geneva
UN Relief and Works Agency for Palestine Refugees in the Near East	UNRWA	established by General Assembly	Beirut

Agency	Abbreviation	Status	Headquarters
Universal Postal Union	UPU	specialised agency	Berne
World Health Organisation	WHO	specialised agency	Geneva
World Meteorological Organisation	WMO	specialised agency	Geneva

It is not necessary that the man-in-the-street should remember the details of all these agencies. But broadly speaking they are responsible either for international co-ordination in technical matters, or for assistance to the underprivileged peoples of the world, or in a few cases for a combination of both. The Universal Postal Union, for example, is in the main a co-ordinating body. The states and territories which belong to the Union are regarded as forming a single postal region in which mail is handled on a reciprocal basis. All member-countries accept standard regulations for charges, weights, and sizes for mail, and there are additional agreements for the more complicated postal services such as cash-on-delivery parcels. The Universal Postal Union is one of the smaller United Nations agencies, with a regular staff of forty-three and a net annual budget of about $814,000 (1962).*

An example of the "assistance" type of agency is the United Nations Relief and Works Agency for Palestine Refugees in the Near East, which is responsible for the care of more than one million refugees, and their children, who left Palestine after the Arab-Israeli fighting in 1948 and are now living in the Gaza area, Jordan, Syria, and Lebanon. This body spends about $36 million every year.

The cost to the ordinary citizen of activities of this kind can be expressed in various ways. A citizen of a typical European country contributes about three pence a century for the Universal Postal Union. United Nations care of Arab refugees from Palestine costs each American taxpayer about 15 cents a year. Britain's share of the ordinary annual budget of the United Nations is one-thousandth of her annual expenditure on military defence.

* United Nations accounts are kept in dollars. For a rough conversion of US dollars to pounds sterling, multiply by 7, then divide by 2, and cancel the last figure, e.g. $40 × 7 = 280; 280 ÷ 2 = 140; cancel last figure = £14.

The demands of the United Nations are likely to increase. A world organisation based on humanitarian principles cannot neglect the victims of man's inhumanity—slaves, for example, or refugees. The United Nations must strive to contain crises which might erupt into war.

The pace of history is fast, and the world has changed radically since the United Nations was founded in 1945. The development of weapons capable of massive destruction has shaken the pre-nuclear assumption that war could be simply an instrument of politics, a continuation of diplomacy by other means. The deterrent may not always deter; governments do not always act wisely or rationally. There is no easy escape from the risks of war by accident, misunderstanding, or miscalculation. The major powers have in their armouries too many weapons which are more effective if used first than second. The rapid obsolescence of weapons-systems induces a frantic search for a technological break-through, so that to win the arms race is in danger of becoming an end in itself.

Those who created the United Nations could not foresee the technological advances of the nuclear age, but war with the weapons we now call "conventional" was already barbaric when the San Francisco conference met in the spring of 1945. The aim now should not be to make war more civilised; it should be to abolish it.

The San Francisco Charter, even in theory, was not without flaws; in practice, difficulties have arisen which seem not to have been foreseen when the Charter was drafted. There is not yet an international agreement for even partial disarmament, although serious negotiations have taken place. The Charter's plan for the collective use of armed force in the event of aggression broke down at an early date when the great powers failed to agree on how the provisions of the Charter should be implemented; as a consequence, *ad hoc* arrangements for the use of force under the aegis of the United Nations have had to be made.

The process of decolonisation has had an important effect on the working of the United Nations. The need for the process was foreseen in 1945, but not its speed. Its most spectacular manifestation for the United Nations has been in the changed composition of the General Assembly. In 1945, the member-states from Asia and Africa numbered twelve; at the beginning of 1963, they numbered fifty-seven. This has meant a radical shift in the balance of votes in United Nations organs, and the countries of the Afro-Asian area are now in a majority. These countries are not always in agreement and, in any case, decisions of the General Assembly on important questions require a two-thirds vote. But the situation is that neither the Soviet bloc nor the West can win an important vote in the General Assembly without the support of a majority of Afro-Asian states. The Cold War in the United Nations has increasingly become a matter of rival blocs' wooing the onlookers rather than scowling at each other.

TABLE II

UNITED NATIONS MEMBERSHIP, 1945–62

	Western Europe	Eastern Europe	Asia and Africa	Oceania	The Americas	Total
Founder members	9	6	12	2	22	51
Admissions during						
1946	2	—	2	—	—	4
1947	—	—	2	—	—	2
1948	—	—	1	—	—	1
1949	—	—	1	—	—	1
1950	—	—	1	—	—	1
1951	—	—	—	—	—	—
1952	—	—	—	—	—	—
1953	—	—	—	—	—	—
1954	—	—	—	—	—	—
1955	6	4	6	—	—	16
1956	—	—	4	—	—	4
1957	—	—	2	—	—	2
1958	—	—	1	—	—	1
1959	—	—	—	—	—	—
1960	—	—	17	—	—	17
1961	—	—	4	—	—	4
1962	—	—	4	—	2	6
Total	17	10	57	2	24	110

The doubling of the Organisation's membership has meant that business takes longer; sessions of the General Assembly now last months rather than weeks. It is not that representatives of the new states are especially long-winded but simply that there are more than twice as many members now as there were in 1945. But the most important consequence of the changed composition of the United Nations lies not in the fact of numbers but in the character and interests of the new states.

Most of these countries are former dependencies of Western powers. They are proud of their new nationhood. They are relatively underdeveloped, but determined to achieve in decades the social and economic advance which in the West took centuries. They are apprehensive lest the Cold War should get out of hand, but they take advantage of great power rivalry to promote their own interests. They are fed up with the bland assumption that the world should be run according to Western ideas and principles.

They are not powerful in the conventional sense, though many of them hope to become powerful in course of time. It is not surprising that they should place their hopes in the United Nations, which seeks to minimise the role of national military power, and that they should use the Organisation to promote the advancement of the needy parts of the world.

It is sometimes said that the concentration of votes in the hands of relatively weak countries distorts the realities of the international situation. The traditional theory has been that power should be used to enforce justice and right, though it was never possible to ensure that only the righteous would take the sword. The lack of correlation between votes and power is often a problem, but it is relatively insignificant compared with the lack of correlation between power and a sense of international responsibility.

There can be no guarantee that there will not be an occasional vote in the General Assembly of which it can justly be charged that the majority comprised a coalition of the weak and the irresponsible. This is a risk inherent in any political system which uses voting as a means of deciding a disputed question.

The use of voting to settle international questions is one manifestation of what Dean Rusk has called "parliamentary diplomacy". "Parliamentary diplomacy", suggests Mr. Rusk, is a form of multilateral negotiation which has the following characteristics distinguishing it from traditional diplomacy. First, the idea of public debate, terminating in a formal conclusion normally reached by voting. Secondly, a continuing organisation with interests and responsibilities broader than the specific items which happen to appear on the agenda at any particular time. Thirdly, the use of rules of procedure which are subject to tactical manipulation to advance or oppose a point of view.

The General Assembly may resemble a parliament, but a parliament of the days when there was no stable party-system, no notion that the cabinet should be responsible to the legislature, and no thought that the representative character of the legislature should be ensured by democratic elections.

The "parliamentary" diplomacy of the General Assembly differs greatly from traditional diplomacy. The essence of old-style diplomacy was that it was invariably conducted in private; decisions required the unanimous support or acquiescence of all the parties concerned. "Parliamentary" diplomacy is much more public—although it is rarely successful unless what takes place in public is reinforced by private exchanges of various kinds. And the normal way of disposing of a matter in "parliamentary" diplomacy is by voting.

A vote is useful to the extent that it either registers agreement already reached or induces a situation in which agreement is more likely in the future. A vote which merely records a difference of opinion serves little useful purpose—except, perhaps, to enable the body concerned to proceed to the next item of business. A recommendation of the General Assembly which is accepted by everyone except the government or governments to which it is directed may lull uneasy consciences; it may assert important principles; it may create an impression that progress has been made; but it has failed in an essential purpose if it has not helped to modify the views, or at least the policies, of those responsible for the situation which has aroused concern.

The fact is that debate is often more important than the vote with which it normally terminates. Public debate enables a country to "put the record straight", as the saying is, to state before the world its grievances and ambitions, its hopes and fears. Charges can be denied, claims asserted, accusations rebutted, initiatives launched. The snag is that a speech designed to demonstrate to an unsophisticated electorate at home that a government is not lax in pursuing the national interest is not necessarily suited to achieving another aspect of the national purpose, that is to say, to persuade others to modify their policies. Speeches in United Nations organs too often express extreme views in extravagant language, so that differences become sharper and more crystallised.

Disgust with some of the consequences of old-style secret diplomacy has caused a reaction in parts of the world which, if carried to excess, could have damaging consequences. The United Nations could be brought into contempt, not because debate is harmful, but because obsession with the more public manifestations of "parliamentary" diplomacy distracts attention from the real potentialities which the Organisation provides for reconciling differences and promoting agreement.

Public opinion is nowadays concerned with international affairs to an extent which would have astonished the diplomats who gathered at the Congress of Vienna a century and a half ago. In an era in which war is total, no intelligent person can be indifferent to the means for its avoidance. Tension anywhere endangers men and women everywhere. But a new aspect of diplomacy since the first world war has been that it is often directed over the heads of governments to the people of foreign countries. Leon Trotsky claimed, at the Brest-Litovsk negotiations between Russia and the Central Powers in 1918, that his words were not spoken to the diplomats across the table but to "the war-weary workers of all countries".

All the media of mass communication are now used by governments to influence foreign opinion. This is, perhaps, only a revival of what was normal practice in ancient Greece. Thucydides, in his history of the war between Athens and Sparta in the fifth century before the Christian era, gives several examples of a diplomatic envoy stating his case directly to the people of another state.

Of all aspects of politics, international affairs seem to the ordinary citizen most puzzling. We do not always have adequate information about the outside world until a crisis blows up, or the information we do have is one-sided. Foreigners are difficult to understand; they pig-headedly pursue their own interests, perhaps at our expense. Most of us do not experience directly the consequences of an international dispute until it is getting out of hand. Yet ordinary people everywhere care deeply for peace and would make sacrifices to achieve it.

There is, in fact, no way of buying peace cheaply. All one can say with certainty is that the alternative costs more.

CHAPTER II

STRUCTURE

THE United Nations was set up, as a successor to the League of Nations, by the victors in the second world war. Only those states which declared war on the Axis powers were invited to the founding conference. The Soviet government had earlier asked that the sixteen republics constituting the Soviet Union should have separate membership in the United Nations. President Roosevelt opposed this by saying he would ask for membership for the forty-eight states forming the United States. At the "summit" conference at Yalta in February 1945, the Soviet Union agreed to modify its original demand and to accept three seats in the Organisation, in exchange for American concessions regarding the veto in the Security Council. In addition to the USSR, therefore, the Byelorussian and Ukrainian Soviet Socialist Republics became founding members of the United Nations. Fifty delegations participated in the San Francisco conference, and Poland subsequently became an "original" member of the Organisation.

The San Francisco conference was formally sponsored by the United States, Britain, China and the Soviet Union, and these four states submitted a draft Charter which had been prepared at a preliminary conference at Dumbarton Oaks. France was invited to be a "sponsoring power" at San Francisco but declined. General de Gaulle was piqued at not having been invited to the Yalta conference, and France had not shared in drafting the Dumbarton Oaks Proposals.

The San Francisco conference opened on 25 April 1945, the day on which Western and Soviet troops met on the Elbe;

within ten days, Germany had surrendered. Two months later, the Charter was ready for signature.

The Charter provided that membership in the United Nations would be open to all peace-loving states which accept the obligations of the Charter and, "in the judgment of the Organisation, are able and willing to carry out these obligations". Admission, suspension, and expulsion of members was to be by "the General Assembly upon the recommendation of the Security Council", and decisions on membership were to require the affirmative votes of the five permanent members in the Security Council and a two-thirds majority in the General Assembly. Membership, in other words, was to be one of the matters requiring great power unanimity.

There have been three phases regarding United Nations membership. In the first period (1946–50), nine new members were admitted: Afghanistan, Iceland, Sweden, and Thailand (Siam) in 1946, Pakistan and Yemen in 1947, Burma in 1948, Israel in 1949, and Indonesia in 1950. Membership was, however, increasingly becoming a Cold War issue, with Western-sponsored applications encountering a Soviet veto, and Western countries refusing to vote for the admission of states with communist governments. The deadlock was broken in December 1955 with a package deal. Four states with communist governments, six states of Western Europe, and six Afro-Asian countries were admitted together, bringing the total membership at that date to seventy-six. Since 1955, most countries attaining independence have been admitted automatically; by the beginning of 1963, the membership had reached one hundred-and-ten.

It has been argued that because the United Nations is committed to certain high principles of international conduct, only those states clearly willing to accept and honour the obligations of the Charter qualify for membership. The United Nations, according to this view, should be a club. Nobody should be compelled to join; standards for admission should be high.

Others have held that this is fine in theory, but that in practice the United Nations cannot function effectively without the participation of all, or virtually all, states in the world. They argue further that many of the founding members have not consistently lived up to the high standards of the Charter.

The only test of the suitability of an applicant, they say, should be whether or not it is a state.

The second view has increasingly come to prevail since the package-deal of 1955. It is still a matter of form for a state applying for admission to declare that it accepts the obligations of the Charter, but there is no serious attempt to judge the ability or willingness of the applicant state to carry out these obligations. The Security Council, normally without much debate, adopts a resolution along the following lines.

The Security Council,
Having examined the application of ...
Recommends to the General Assembly that ... be admitted to membership in the United Nations.

The General Assembly, on a convenient occasion, receives the recommendation and, by acclamation, admits the state to membership.

Most sovereign states belong to the United Nations. Switzerland has not applied to join, believing that membership involves an obligation to use collective force against aggression which is inconsistent with Swiss neutrality. The two governments in Korea and the two governments in Vietnam have applied for membership but have not been admitted; neither government in Germany has applied. Kuwait's application for membership ran into a Soviet veto (1961).* China is represented by the nationalist government now in Taiwan (Formosa), so that the People's Republic of China (Peking) is not represented in the United Nations.

The "Republic of China" is a founding member of the United Nations and a permanent member of the Security Council. When the nationalist government was driven from the Chinese mainland and took refuge in Taiwan, the question was bound to arise whether China should in future be represented in United Nations organs by the new communist government in Peking or the nationalist government in Taipeh. This question has both political and constitutional aspects; the political arguments have gone something like this.

The United States, supported by many of its allies, has maintained that the Peking government does not represent the true will and aspirations of the Chinese people. It has shown

* See Appendix III, page 128.

brutality and lack of morality. It committed aggression in Korea, destroyed the autonomy of Tibet, invaded India, fostered subversion in South-east Asia and elsewhere, and threatened to attack Taiwan. Communist China is not peace-loving; its leaders believe that large-scale war is inevitable. To admit its representatives to the United Nations would disrupt the Organisation, reduce the prospects for successful action against aggression in the future, and be interpreted by free nations everywhere as an abandonment of their cause. Representatives of the nationalist government in Taiwan have served the United Nations loyally and should not be expelled.

The countries of the Soviet bloc, on the other hand, have maintained that the United States has never reconciled itself to the victory of popular revolution in China, but has tried to thwart the will of the Chinese people by depriving China of its rightful place in the United Nations. The United States, it is said, seized Taiwan and turned it into a base for aggression against the People's Republic of China. If American forces were removed from Taiwan, the Chiang Kai-shek regime would be swept aside. The Chinese seat at the United Nations has been occupied by those who represent nobody. The United Nations should have no concern with internal developments in China. All that matters is that China is peace-loving. It has always pursued a policy of peaceful co-existence; it participated in the Bandung Conference and has concluded treaties of friendship and non-aggression with other nations.

Several non-communist governments, including Britain, India, and the Scandinavian countries, hold that the Chinese seat in UN organs should be occupied by representatives of the Chinese People's Republic (Peking) because that government effectively controls the national territory. They insist that the character of the government has no bearing on the question of representation in United Nations organs; other governments have disregarded the obligations of the Charter, but this has not interfered with their membership. If the People's Republic of China represents a threat to world peace, it is preferable for it to be present in the United Nations rather than excluded. To permit China to be represented in the United Nations by the Peking government would not reduce the determination of free countries to defend their independence.

So much for the political issues. The constitutional position is that if the People's Republic of China had specifically applied for United Nations membership, the question of admission would have been considered in the ordinary way by the Security Council and, in the event of a positive recommendation by the Council, by the General Assembly. Such a procedure might, of course, have run into a veto in the Security Council. In the absence of an application for membership from Peking, however, the issue has generally been regarded as one of representation rather than membership: which government, in other words, is entitled to issue credentials for "the Republic of China".

During the period 1950–60, the General Assembly decided by majority vote each year that it would not even consider the question of Chinese representation. In 1961, the General Assembly decided that it would consider the matter, and decided also that any proposal to change the representation of China was an "important" matter and therefore required a two-thirds majority vote. In 1961, and again in 1962, the General Assembly rejected proposals to replace representatives of the nationalists in Taiwan by representatives of the communists in Peking.

All members of the United Nations are automatically members of the General Assembly. The General Assembly convenes for its ordinary annual session in September; if, as is now usually the case, business is not completed by about the third week in December, the session resumes the following spring. The General Assembly meets in plenary meeting to elect officers and for other procedural business, and for a general debate lasting about five weeks. A representative committee of the Assembly reviews all proposals to place items on the agenda, makes recommendations regarding the date for adjourning or closing the session, and assists the President of the Assembly in the discharge of his responsibilities.

Most substantive items of the agenda requiring debate and decision are considered in public in one or other of seven committees of the whole membership. Procedure in these committees is less formal than in the plenary. Representatives speak seated at their desks rather than standing at a rostrum at the front, and voting is by simple majority. All recommendations approved in the committees are later considered in the plenary, where a two-thirds vote is necessary for deciding important questions.

The General Assembly transacts three types of business:

(i) In a few matters, the Assembly has exclusive authority; the most important of these are control of the budget and apportionment of the expenses of the United Nations, and elections to the three Councils.

(ii) In certain other matters, the Assembly acts in conjunction with the Security Council; these matters include the appointment of the Secretary-General, United Nations membership, amendments to the Charter, and the election of judges of the International Court.

(iii) In addition, the Assembly has wide powers of debate concerning matters within the scope of the Charter, and the right to make recommendations or express opinions.

Of the three UN Councils, the *Security Council* is probably the best known. It consists of five permanent members (the United States, the Soviet Union, China, Britain, and France), each with the right of veto on most kinds of substantive decision, and six other members elected by the General Assembly. The Security Council is in theory very powerful. All members of the United Nations have agreed that the Council has "primary responsibility" for maintaining peace and acts on their behalf, and all have undertaken to accept and carry out all its decisions.

The Council is able to meet at short notice; indeed, the Charter states that it shall be so organised as to be able to "function continuously". It is laid down in the rules of procedure that the Council shall meet at least once every fourteen days, but the rule is not observed in practice. The Council has, however, held more than one thousand meetings since the United Nations was founded. It meets at United Nations headquarters in New York, but it could meet elsewhere if it so decided.

In all important United Nations organs, simultaneous interpretation by headphones is provided by the Secretariat into the five official languages: English, Russian, French, Spanish, and Chinese. The Security Council uses this method of simultaneous interpretation, but it is also provided with subsequent and less hurried consecutive interpretation into English,

French, and Russian. This slows down proceedings, but provides the opportunity for private discussions and negotiations.

The most distinctive feature of the Security Council, however, is that it is the only United Nations organ in which there is a formal rule of unanimity or right of veto. The Charter declares that decisions of the Council shall be by the affirmative vote of seven members and that, except for procedural matters, the seven votes shall include "the concurring votes of the [five] permanent members". The one exception to this Charter rule is that in decisions relating to the pacific settlement of disputes, "a party to a dispute shall abstain from voting". If seven or more of the eleven members vote in favour of a proposal but one of the five permanent members votes "no", the proposal is defeated. Strictly speaking, an abstention should count as a veto, but the practice has been to regard only negative votes as vetoes.

The largest of the three UN Councils is that concerned with economic and social affairs: the *Economic and Social Council*. Often abbreviated to ECOSOC, it should not be confused with UNESCO, the specialised agency of the United Nations concerned with education, science, and culture.

ECOSOC has eighteen members, all elected by the General Assembly. Efforts are made to distribute seats among the whole membership of the United Nations on an equitable basis, although this is not required by the Charter. ECOSOC has two main sessions a year, one in the spring, usually at United Nations headquarters in New York and lasting two to three weeks, and one in the summer in Geneva lasting four to five weeks.

The Economic and Social Council has important coordinating responsibilities. It has established a variety of regional and functional commissions and other bodies, and it is also empowered by the Charter to "co-ordinate the activities of the specialised agencies". ECOSOC considers general policy questions regarding economic and social development, and makes recommendations.

One interesting feature of the Economic and Social Council is that it is authorised by the Charter to "make suitable arrangements for consultation with non-governmental organisations". Being itself concerned with international questions,

ECOSOC has naturally granted consultative status mainly to international rather than national non-official agencies. Representatives of these non-governmental bodies are given facilities to follow closely the work of ECOSOC and its subsidiary organs. They receive documents, have access to meetings, and may in certain circumstances submit oral or written statements giving the experience or views of their organisation. Thus, religious representatives have made statements about religious liberty, trade union representatives about forced labour, business representatives about international trade.

There is clearly a role for these non-governmental organisations so long as they do not try to usurp the functions of governments. In some matters, non-governmental bodies have direct experience and knowledge which official bodies cannot have. There are, for example, several non-governmental organisations with many years of first-hand experience of dealing with refugees, and this experience can be useful to appropriate organs of the United Nations.

The third UN Council, the *Trusteeship Council*, has two distinctive features of interest. First, it was decided at San Francisco that membership of the Trusteeship Council should be divided equally between states which administer trust territories and states which do not. There would thus be a voting balance, so that neither "side" would be able to force through the Council a decision unacceptable to the other "side". The Charter provided that the Council should consist of:

(i) states administering trust territories;
(ii) those of the five permanent members of the Security Council not administering trust territories, together with as many other members elected by the General Assembly as might be necessary to ensure that the Council would be equally divided between states which administer trust territories and those which do not.

The balance within the Council which the Charter had intended to provide worked satisfactorily until 1960. A difficulty was then encountered because no arrangements had been included in the Charter to deal with the situation which would arise as trust territories achieved independence. After two trust territories in Africa which had previously been administered by France (Cameroons and Togoland) became independent, France continued as a member of the Council, but thereafter as a non-administering member. Thus the non-colonial "side" included a colonial power.

But the situation was destined to become even more complicated, because the time would come when the number of states administering trust territories would be fewer than the number of permanent members of the Security Council not administering trust territories. In such circumstances, there would be no way within the Charter of constituting the Council on a basis of parity.

The second interesting feature of the Trusteeship Council is that it is the only organ for which specific provision was made in the Charter for the receipt of petitions. Individuals and organisations may petition the Council directly about conditions in trust territories, and in fact the volume of petitions and other communications has sometimes been so great as to threaten to overwhelm the machinery of the United Nations.

The General Assembly and the three Councils may set up subsidiary organs, especially for detailed studies between sessions of the parent body. Subsidiary organs may consist of governmental representatives (being identical in composition with the parent body, or consisting of a limited membership selected from the parent body, or occasionally having a larger membership than the parent body); or subsidiary organs may consist of persons appointed in their individual capacities (either a single individual or several persons).

Subsidiary organs set up for special purposes lapse when the work is completed; others are standing bodies and remain in being indefinitely. The commission to investigate the death of Dag Hammarskjöld and the other members of the party accompanying him was an example of a temporary body. It was set up by the General Assembly in October 1961, and it completed its work with the submission of its findings six months later. An example of a standing body is the Commission on Human Rights, which was set up by ECOSOC in 1946 and is still at work.

The Economic and Social Council and the Trusteeship Council operate "under the authority of the General Assembly", but the Assembly has no authority over the

Security Council. The Security Council has primary responsibility for maintaining world peace and security, and the Charter provides that while the Security Council is exercising the functions assigned to it in the Charter in respect of any dispute or situation, the General Assembly "shall not make any recommendations with regard to that dispute or situation". It was apparently thought at San Francisco that this would make it impossible for the two organs to deal concurrently with the same question. In practice, however, the General Assembly has not been inclined to allow this provision of the Charter to limit its freedom to any considerable extent. For one thing, the Assembly may *discuss* a matter which is before the Security Council; the prohibition is on the making of recommendations. Secondly, there is always room for argument about the precise meaning of the words: "While the Security Council is exercising . . . the functions assigned to it in the . . . Charter". It can be argued that the fact that a matter is on the agenda of the Security Council does not, of itself, constitute the exercise of functions. Finally, the Assembly has sometimes been able to take up a matter, or an aspect of a matter, with which the Security Council has been concerned by claiming that what it is in fact considering is in some respects different from the matter which had been before the Council. Thus the Assembly on several occasions considered the Indonesian claim to West New Guinea (West Irian) although an item entitled "The Indonesian Question" had been on the agenda of the Security Council since 1946.

The Assembly and the three Councils consist of states; the two other principal organs of the United Nations (the Secretariat and the International Court) consist of individuals. The Secretariat comprises a Secretary-General appointed by the General Assembly on the recommendation of the Security Council, and other staff appointed by the Secretary-General. All staff members are supposed to act as international officials, responsible only to the United Nations, and should at all times be independent of all authorities external to the Organisation. The paramount consideration in the employment of staff is the necessity of securing the highest standards of performance and integrity, but due regard is also to be paid to the importance of recruiting on as wide a geographical basis as possible.

The Secretariat services the policy-making organs, and the Secretary-General performs whatever other functions may be entrusted to him by these organs. In addition, the Secretary-General has the specific right to "bring to the attention of the Security Council" any matter which in his opinion may threaten world peace and security.

One of the most significant developments since the United Nations was founded has been the tendency to entrust the Secretariat with important responsibilities. To some extent this reflects an enlarged conception of the functions which states regard it as proper for an international organisation to undertake. But in addition there have been two other factors at work. First, the policy-making bodies have entrusted the Secretaries-General with important political tasks, although the mandates have often been expressed in general terms, allowing considerable latitude regarding interpretation and implementation. Secondly, the Secretaries-General have considered it within the letter and spirit of the Charter to take independent initiatives designed to safeguard world peace. Dissatisfaction within the Soviet bloc about Dag Hammarskjöld's initiatives and interpretations of Security Council resolutions regarding the Congo led to the *troika* proposal for tripartite administration.

The other principal organ of the United Nations, the International Court of Justice, has its seat at The Hague. The Court consists of fifteen independent judges elected regardless of nationality from among persons of high moral character and who have the highest judicial qualifications. The election should be conducted so that the main forms of civilisation and the principal legal systems of the world are represented. It is unnecessary to describe here the complicated procedures of nomination and election, except to say that the election of judges is a joint responsibility of the Security Council and the General Assembly, and that an absolute majority of votes is needed in both organs. It is interesting to note that there is an apparent inconsistency between the Statute of the Court and the Charter of the United Nations on this point; the Statute refers to "an absolute majority of votes . . . in the Security Council" (that is to say, six out of eleven), whereas the Charter refers to "an affirmative vote of seven members".

Only states may be parties to contentious cases before the Court, but states are not under an obligation to submit cases for settlement. However, states may accept the compulsory jurisdiction of the Court, either unconditionally or on condition of reciprocity on the part of other states. Each member of the United Nations undertakes to comply with the decision of the Court in any case to which it is a party. The Court may, at the request of other United Nations organs, give advisory opinions on legal questions.

The Court is in permanent session, except for judicial vacations, and may sit at The Hague or elsewhere as needed. It elects its own President and Vice-President, and appoints a Registrar and other officers. Decisions of the Court are taken

TABLE III

COMPOSITION OF THE SIX PRINCIPAL ORGANS

Organ	Composition	Method of election or appointment	
General Assembly	All the members of the United Nations	—	Charter Art. 9(1)
Security Council	(i) Five permanent members: Republic of China, France, Soviet Union, United Kingdom, and United States of America	—	Art. 23(1)
	(ii) Six non-permanent members	Election by General Assembly, due regard being specially paid in the first instance to the contribution of members to the maintenance of international peace and security and the other purposes of the United Nations, and also to equitable geographical distribution	Art. 23(1)
Economic and Social Council	Eighteen members	Election by General Assembly	Art. 61

Organ	Composition	Method of election or appointment	
Trusteeship Council	(i) Members administering trust territories	—	Art. 86(1)(a)
	(ii) Those of the five permanent members of the Security Council not administering trust territories	—	Art. 86(1)(b)
	(iii) As many other members as may be necessary to ensure that the total number of members of the Council is equally divided between members of the UN which administer trust territories and those which do not	Election by General Assembly	Art. 86(1)(c)
Secretariat	(i) Secretary-General	Appointment by General Assembly upon recommendation of Security Council	Art. 97
	(ii) Other staff	Appointment by Secretary-General under regulations established by General Assembly. The paramount consideration of employment of staff shall be the necessity of securing the highest standards of efficiency, competence and integrity. Due regard shall be paid to the importance of recruiting staff on as wide a geographical basis as possible	Art. 101(1) and (3)

Organ	Composition	*Method of election or appointment*	
International Court of Justice	Fifteen independent judges	Election by General Assembly and Security Council. The Court shall be composed of judges elected regardless of nationality from among persons of high moral character, and who have the highest judicial qualifications. The persons elected should individually possess the qualifications required; and in the Court as a whole the representation of the main forms of civilisation and of the principal legal systems of the world should be assured	Statute Arts. 2–4, 8–15

in private by majority vote, the quorum being nine, and any judge is entitled to deliver a separate opinion. The judgment of the Court must state the reasons on which it is based.

The organisation and structure described in this chapter derive, in the main, from the Charter. To amend the Charter, there must be a favourable vote of two-thirds of the members of the United Nations, including all five permanent members of the Security Council. But the fact that the United Nations Charter cannot easily be amended has not prevented considerable adjustment of practice within the Charter's general framework. In at least one instance, indeed, there has been a tacit agreement that the words of the Charter shall be interpreted in a way quite contrary to their apparent meaning.

The article of the Charter dealing with voting in the Security Council states that decisions on non-procedural matters "shall be made by an affirmative vote of seven members including the concurring votes of the [five] permanent members". The plain man would not regard this statement as ambiguous. It means, or appears to mean, that one of the permanent members of the Council can block a decision simply by failing to vote "yes". A negative vote, or an abstention, or non-participation in the vote, or absence from the Council—any of these methods, it might be thought, could be used to prevent a decision. But in practice, only a negative vote by a permanent member has been regarded as a veto. There has been no formal proposal to bring the Charter into line with practice. Governments have evidently been content to let things slide, realising that it would probably be impossible to amend one article of the Charter without reviewing all the articles which have given rise to misunderstanding or controversy.

It would be perfectly possible to tidy up the Charter, eliminating an ambiguity here or an inconsistency there. There is, in fact, a considerable body of opinion favouring an increase in the size of the Security Council and ECOSOC so that the new member-states from Asia and Africa could have larger representation, but the countries of the Soviet bloc have opposed even limited revision of the Charter until the Peking government is properly represented in United Nations organs.

The one apparent exception to the general Soviet position on Charter revision relates to the Secretariat. The Soviet *troika* proposal would replace a single Secretary-General by a collective body comprising a representative of the Soviet bloc, a representative of Western states, and a representative of neutral countries. N. S. Khrushchev, in presenting the proposal in 1960, said that such a three-man executive would correspond to the realities of the world and would prevent decisions being implemented by the Secretariat in a manner detrimental to the interests of a particular group of states.

Although some aspects of the *troika* proposal have not been fully elucidated, it is generally understood that it would have two important consequences. First, in certain circumstances a member of the three-man board would have the power to block executive action, either by outright veto or by delaying tactics. Secondly, the *troika* would increase the political character of the Secretariat by formally introducing the idea that staff members have a duty to "represent" national or bloc policies. The *troika* would thus change the idea, stated in the Charter, that the Secretariat is composed of international officials whose exclusive loyalty is to the United Nations. The countries of the Soviet bloc claim that this is an impossible ideal, that in the last resort there are no neutral men.

The *troika* idea did not make headway when it was first put forward in 1960 or during the weeks following Hammarskjöld's death in 1961. The Western countries firmly opposed it, arguing that if Soviet complaints about the Secretariat were legitimate, they could be met without extending the veto and without abandoning the principle of an impartial and independent staff. The neutral and uncommitted countries were also opposed to the *troika* in the form in which it was presented, although there was some sentiment, particularly among African and Asian governments, that there ought to be some modification of the top-level organisation of the Secretariat.

Hammarskjöld's death was followed by an anxious period of intensive negotiation about the future of the office of Secretary-General. There was a widespread desire that Hammarskjöld should be succeeded by an independent Secretary-General, preferably from one of the neutral countries of Asia or Africa, appointed according to the procedure laid down in the Charter. The decision to appoint U Thant as Acting Secretary-General in 1961, and as Secretary-General a year later, was unanimous in both the Security Council and the General Assembly.

U Thant has named eight Under-Secretaries as special advisers, and he consults them, individually or collectively, as he sees fit. His formal independence is preserved; the eight advisers are members of the Secretariat, owing allegiance to the United Nations and not "representing" ideologies or regions.

Throughout the discussions of 1960–61, and indeed earlier, considerable dissatisfaction had been expressed about the geographical composition of the Secretariat. Recruitment in the early days had been mainly from those Western countries best able to spare qualified personnel. During the early post-war period, the East European member-states showed little enthusiasm to release a significant number of persons to serve in the Secretariat, and few of the countries of Asia, the Middle East, Africa, or Latin America were able to spare suitably qualified staff. In 1946, 83 per cent of the professional staff at headquarters (other than linguists) were from Western countries.

With the admission to the United Nations of new Asian and African members. and with a growing realisation of the important role which the Secretariat plays, pressure to increase the recruitment of non-Westerners has grown. A rough quota system for recruitment was established in 1948, and the initial imbalance has been partially corrected. Between 1946 and 1962, the number of professional staff from Eastern Europe increased from 7 per cent to 10 per cent, the Latin Americans from 4 per cent to 9 per cent, and the number from the Afro-Asian area from 6 per cent to 24 per cent. This has been at the price of some damage to the concept of an international career service based on merit alone, and has also involved an increase in the number of seconded short-term officials.

The idea of an impartial and non-partisan civil service is not universally accepted. In many member-states, the distinction between politics and administration is blurred. But the Charter is clear. Whatever views a particular staff-member may hold in private, whatever the character of the government of the country of which he happens to be a citizen, so long as he is employed in the United Nations Secretariat, his whole loyalty should be to the United Nations. If he cannot conscientiously take the oath or declaration of loyalty, he should not masquerade as an international official.

CHAPTER III

GROUPINGS

SOME of the more optimistic speeches at San Francisco in 1945 seemed to suggest that the United Nations, simply by existing, would put an end to all international conflict. While it is legitimate to hope for the best, it is only realistic to assume that disputes between nations and between groups of nations will continue for the foreseeable future. The leaders of the major powers believe that disputes are inevitable, and act accordingly.

Let me refer here to an official publication which reached me from abroad on the day on which this page was written. This document analyses the foreign policy of a country which I will call X. One of the key facts about country X, says the writer, is the belief of their people that the world is divided into two hostile groupings which are contending for world leadership. The people of country X, he writes, consider that this competition will continue until one system or the other emerges triumphant. In this struggle, the tactics of country X are determined largely by considerations of military power. We must keep up our strength, and this will eventually induce them to moderate their hostility.

Now what strikes one as interesting about this is that one cannot identify country X with certainty. A Westerner would probably take it for granted that X equals Russia or China. A communist, on the other hand, would be just as likely to regard X as being the United States.

This is not the place to attempt to analyse the reasons for the competition between the Soviet bloc and the West. Suffice it to say that this competition has caused or complicated almost every international crisis since the United Nations was founded. The United Nations has been a forum in which the struggle has been pursued, and there have been times when the struggle has seemed to assume greater importance than the ends for which it is ostensibly waged.

There were some who hoped that the system of collective security laid down in the Charter would make it unnecessary for states to enter into military alliances. It is true that the Charter declares that "regional arrangements or agencies" consistent with the principles and purposes of the United Nations are permitted, but this was not to impair the primary responsibility of the Security Council for dealing with international disputes or threatening situations. The fact that the Charter made provision for regional arrangements seems to have been due to Churchill's enthusiasm during the war for a United Nations based on strong regional groupings.

The plan for collective measures by the United Nations in the event of threats to peace or acts of aggression, inadequate though it may be in theory, has never been properly implemented in practice because of disagreement about the nature and control of the national forces which were to be placed at the disposal of the Security Council. In the absence of a reliable United Nations system of security, states have entered into such military alliances as NATO and the Warsaw Pact.

Much may be said about alliances of this kind, but I want to stress four points here. First, they were created in the belief that the United Nations system was inadequate. Secondly, they do not seem in practice to conform to all the requirements of the Charter; it is, for example, laid down in the Charter that the Security Council shall at all times be kept fully informed of activities undertaken or in contemplation under regional arrangements or by regional agencies for the maintenance of international peace and security—an obligation which has not been properly and consistently observed. Thirdly, all members of the United Nations have expressly agreed that their obligations under the UN Charter prevail over their obligations under other international agreements. Fourthly, limited alliances tend to induce habits of thought and vested interests inimical to the development in the future of a sound system of collective security on a universal basis. Although such a goal may now seem far beyond our reach, we should recognise that some of the steps taken in the hope of preserving peace in the short run make the long-term goal seem even more utopian than would otherwise be the case.

If the United Nations cannot at present provide a fool-proof system of security, it can at least seek to soften the harsh edges of controversy and conflict. And here we encounter a paradox, for the processes of "parliamentary" diplomacy which have evolved in the United Nations often have contrary effects. On the one hand, the informal aspects of "parliamentary" diplomacy can most certainly help to remove misunderstanding and foster agreement. There is constant discussion and negotiation in the lobbies. Representatives of more than one hundred countries meet casually or by arrangement almost every day of the year at United Nations headquarters in New York—relax in the same lounge, eat in the same dining-room, patronise the same barber. Many of these men and women acquire a professional pride in the United Nations as an institution, a sense of solidarity and common purpose. I do not wish to exaggerate either the extent or the importance of the personal understanding which can develop across political barriers, but it undoubtedly facilitates the conduct of contemporary diplomacy.

A negative side of the coin is that "parliamentary" diplomacy constantly forces countries to take sides. It is taken for granted that debate is merely a prelude to a vote; it is often said that states have a duty to stand up and be counted. Nine times out of ten, to be sure, a vote is necessary; it would be impossible to conduct the business of the United Nations without voting. All the same, issues have sometimes been brought to an unnecessary or premature vote, thereby exacerbating rather than relieving the tension.

The fact that a quasi-parliamentary process is at work in the United Nations fosters some of the manifestations which we tend to associate with an ordinary party system—caucuses, whips, slates of candidates, lobbies, horse-trading, log-rolling, and the like. Some of this diplomatic manoeuvring takes place on an *ad hoc* basis in the various capitals, but it is mainly centred in New York, and to a lesser extent in Geneva. Just as political parties within a nation emerged when individuals put aside differences of detail in order to act unitedly for larger ends, so nations associate in pursuit of their common interests.

Ordinary meetings of UN organs, except for those of the Security Council, take place according to a prearranged schedule. But the Charter requires that the Security Council shall be so organised as to be able to function continuously, and this means in practice that it must always be able to meet at a few hours' notice. The consequence in the early days was that the members of the Security Council had to maintain diplomatic representation in New York on a continuous basis. As UN organs have proliferated and sessions have lengthened, so it has become necessary for virtually all member-states to set up permanent diplomatic missions at UN headquarters, and to supplement these with specialists as required. Some countries which are not members of the United Nations, such as Switzerland, have permanent observers at the United Nations.

In many respects, the permanent missions of member-states correspond to conventional diplomatic missions, but three differences should be noted. *First*, although the Permanent Representative of a member of the United Nations presents credentials to the Secretary-General, he is not accredited to the Secretary-General in the way that an ambassador is accredited to the head of state of the country in which he serves. There is, moreover, no requirement that the Secretary-General should give prior approval to the appointment of a particular person as Permanent Representative. *Secondly,* the permanent mission of a member-state has responsibilities regarding the United Nations but not for relations with the host-country; these are handled separately in Washington or Berne rather than in New York or Geneva. *Thirdly*, persons on the staff of national missions to the United Nations need qualifications additional to those normally expected of foreign service officers. A UN delegate is, in a sense, accredited to more than a hundred countries rather than to just one; with some of these his own nation may not have diplomatic relations. A UN delegate must be able to speak clearly and convincingly in public at short notice; he must understand the formal and informal procedures of UN organs and be able to take tactical advantage of unexpected situations; he must establish civilised personal relations with a variety of foreigners, some of whom he may find disagreeable; he must be able to handle representatives of the press.

In order to facilitate the working of multilateral diplomacy, the UN building in New York was designed to be more than simply a series of conference rooms and offices. UN headquarters in New York include lounges and lobbies, dining rooms and snack bars, a library, a post office, a medical clinic, a bank, a travel agency, a bookshop, a barber. The United Nations, being on international territory, employs its own uniformed guards.

On most days of the year, meetings of United Nations organs take place. In addition to the delegates participating in these meetings, other delegates will be present as observers, or to meet colleagues by arrangement, or perhaps just to get the feel of opinion around the United Nations. Groups gather in the delegates' lounge or in quiet corners of the building, and the experienced journalist will speculate as to why ambassador *A* is talking so earnestly to under-secretary *B*, or whether the absence of delegates from a particular regional group means that a caucus is being held. The loud-speakers of the public address system announce in a variety of languages the opening and closing of official UN meetings, or summon individual delegates to speak on the telephone or to meet visitors. The loud-speakers may also announce meetings of delegates which have no official UN status—the blocs and groups.

It would be convenient and tidy if groupings of states at the United Nations corresponded exactly to geographical regions. This would, for example, simplify the application of the Charter requirement that among the criteria for electing states to the Security Council should be "equitable geographical distribution". The problem of implementing this provision would be easier to deal with if the states in each region were sufficiently similar that any one of them could be regarded as broadly representative of the region as a whole. But there are differences within every region.

Consider the Middle East. The region is thought of by many people as Arab and Moslem. It is, indeed, true that the core of the region consists of five Moslem and Arab member-states (Iraq, Jordan, Saudi Arabia, Syria, Yemen), together with one Arab member-state in which Christians are in a slight majority (Lebanon). For many United Nations purposes, however, the Middle East also comprises the United Arab Republic (Egypt), three non-Arab but mainly Moslem states (Afghanistan, Iran, and Turkey), the Jewish state of Israel, and Cyprus which is predominantly Greek-speaking and Orthodox Christian but which includes a Turkish-speaking Moslem minority. Two of the specialised agencies regard Pakistan, part of which has a common frontier with Burma, as in the Middle East.

It has sometimes been urged that the Middle East is such an important region that it should always have one "representative" on the Security Council, but it is one thing to demand this in theory and quite another thing to apply it in practice. Which state can "represent" the Middle East?

This diversity within regions is not just a matter for academic discussion. The great powers reached an informal understanding in 1946 about the distribution of the six members to be elected by the General Assembly to the Security Council. Part of this understanding was that one of the six should be an East European state—although there is disagreement now as to whether the understanding of the great powers was to apply only to the 1946 elections or was to have continuing validity. At any rate, Poland was elected for 1946–7 and the Ukraine for 1948–9, thus maintaining the 1946 understanding. For the period 1950–1, and again for 1956, the General Assembly elected Yugoslavia, a communist state which had broken with the Soviet bloc; Greece was elected to fill the vacancy for 1952–3 and Turkey for 1954–5. The so-called East European seat was later filled by the Philippines (1957 and 1963), Japan (1958–9), and Liberia (1961).

The Soviet government has contended that, apart altogether from the years when there has been no pretence at filling the seat by a state from Eastern Europe (1957–9, 1961 and 1963), the election of countries outside the Soviet bloc to "represent" Eastern Europe is a breach of the spirit if not the letter of the 1946 understanding. The Soviet government favours a system analogous to the "primary" elections in the United States, in which candidates would be selected by the countries of the region concerned. While this procedure would have many unsatisfactory features, it must at least be said that the Security Council cannot discharge the responsibilities entrusted to it unless it is constituted in a broadly representative way. Since five of the seats on the Council are occupied by permanent members, it is most important that the six electoral seats should be equitably distributed.

There are anomalies in all regions. Even if Eastern Europe is regarded, rather arbitrarily, as consisting only of those European states with communist governments, it still does not coincide with the Soviet bloc. Yugoslavia is in Eastern Europe, has had a communist government since the United Nations was founded, and was part of the Soviet bloc until the break with the Cominform in 1948. At the present time, however, Yugoslavia is regarded by more orthodox communist states as "revisionist". Yugoslavia enjoys cordial relations with several of the unaligned countries of Asia and Africa, notably India and the United Arab Republic (Egypt), and acted as host to a conference of neutral nations in 1961. Albania is regarded by the Soviet Union as excessively "dogmatist", and in recent years Albania has been estranged from the Soviet bloc. Outer Mongolia is not in Eastern Europe but is part of the communist bloc and in 1962 was admitted to the Council for Mutual Economic Assistance, the economic counterpart of the Warsaw Pact.

South Africa, Israel, and nationalist China, though from the Afro-Asian geographical region, are not members of the Afro-Asian Group at the United Nations. Cuba, a Latin American state, attended the conference of neutral nations in Belgrade in 1961 and has drawn increasingly close to the communist camp. Turkey is both Middle Eastern and European. She is a member of the Afro-Asian Group, and also a signatory of the North Atlantic Treaty. Turkey has sometimes been considered as part of the Middle East, sometimes as part of Eastern Europe, and sometimes even as part of Western Europe.

All of the informal associations of states at United Nations headquarters, with one exception, call themselves "groups"—a conveniently non-committal word. The countries associated with the Soviet Union call themselves a "bloc". This difference of terminology is useful, because the Soviet bloc does differ from the other groups of states. It is more disciplined than the others, has greater cohesion. It has a recognised leader—the Soviet Union. It shares a common ideology—Marxism. The bloc's European members, except for Albania in recent years, are military allies in the Warsaw Pact and are associated in the Council for Mutual Economic Assistance.

The Soviet bloc countries co-operate closely on both the governmental and the party level.

Members of the Soviet bloc adopt the same public position on all important international questions. It is true that there have been a few occasions on which members of the bloc have failed to vote identically in UN organs, but such rare deviations are nearly always due to misunderstanding. There are sometimes interesting differences in the tone of voice or choice of language of Soviet bloc speakers; Polish delegates, for example, have since 1956 often sounded somewhat less harsh and polemical than Czechoslovak delegates. But these differences of emphasis do not alter the fact that the states of the Soviet bloc present a united front in public on international issues.

Almost nothing is known about the means by which this agreement is reached within the bloc. Their UN delegates are steeped in Marxist ideology and thus share common habits of thought. The Soviet Union, as the first country to undergo a communist revolution and as a country of considerable material power, enjoys a position of special pre-eminence and leadership within the bloc. The states of the Soviet camp believe that countries which have embarked on the road to communism have minimised if not eliminated internal contradictions, so that important differences of foreign policy are inconceivable. But all this, to the non-communist, is a bit enigmatic; it remains true that the outside world can only guess at the processes by which agreement within the Soviet bloc is secured.

Opposed to the Soviet bloc on what are sometimes called "Cold War issues" has been a pro-Western coalition centring around the United States and including the twenty other UN member-states belonging to NATO, CENTO, and SEATO, as well as most of the Latin American countries, Spain, Japan, nationalist China, Israel, and South Africa. This core of about forty-five states is not able to win a vote in the General Assembly without other support. With one hundred-and-ten members of the United Nations, and assuming no abstentions, seventy-four votes are needed to secure a two-thirds majority. It is thus not true, as is sometimes suggested, that the United States has an "automatic'" majority in the Assembly. To win an important vote, the United States must gain the support of more than half the neutral or uncommitted countries.

Within the pro-Western coalition is one fairly homogeneous group which has met regularly as a caucus since the United Nations was founded. Among the fifty-one original members of the United Nations were twenty Latin American republics, bound together by tradition, culture and religion. All these states have Mediterranean affinities; the Roman Catholic religion predominates; all, except Brazil and Haiti, are Spanish-speaking; all, along with the United States, have belonged to the Organisation of American States. As the membership of the United Nations has increased, the relative strength of the Latin American Group has declined from 40 per cent of the original membership to less than 20 per cent at the present time.

The Latin American Group usually meets about once a week while the General Assembly is in session, and about once a month at other times of the year. Voting at meetings of the Group is not usual, but every effort is made to secure substantial agreement on nomination or support of Latin American candidates in UN elections.

The Latin American countries, except for Cuba in recent years, are generally pro-Western in outlook on "Cold War" issues, but they are anti-colonial and in most cases are relatively underdeveloped. While they are not technically neutral, since they have mutual defence arrangements, some of them have sought to exert a moderating influence in UN affairs. Mexico and Brazil have been noteworthy in this regard.

The United Nations members usually thought of as West European comprise the non-communist UN members in Europe, from Iceland to the Eastern Mediterranean. Eleven are members of NATO (twelve if Turkey is included), and Spain has defence arrangements with the United States. There are four West European neutrals: Austria, Finland, Ireland, and Sweden. Within Western Europe are a number of sub-alignments, such as the Nordic countries and those Common Market countries which are members of the United Nations.

The largest association of United Nations members is the Afro-Asian Group which now numbers more than fifty; only eleven of these states were founder-members of the United Nations. The Group drew much of its initial inspiration from the Bandung Conference of 1955, though for some years earlier an informal group of Asian and African countries, fluctuating in composition, had been meeting at UN headquarters for limited purposes.

The Afro-Asian Group meets regularly, the chairmanship rotating. Efforts are made to reach a consensus without voting. India is the largest country in the Group and has often exercised leadership. The Group is by no means always in agreement, but as a generalisation it may be said that the African and Asian countries have stood for the rapid liquidation of the vestiges of colonialism, a large-scale programme of UN aid to the less developed parts of the world, and non-alignment on "Cold War" issues. And because the Group now comprises more than half the votes in the General Assembly, its role is of considerable importance.

The voting situation can be expressed in a number of ways. When the Afro-Asian Group is united on colonial and similar questions, it can almost always pick up enough other votes to get a two-thirds majority; this is also the case with many of the economic and social issues which are pressed to a vote. The overall situation is that the decision of the General Assembly is in most cases that favoured by the majority of the members of the Afro-Asian Group.

The Afro-Asian Group may be regarded as the mouthpiece of those parts of the world which are experiencing the revolution of rising expectations. The third Marquess of Salisbury once described democracy as that system of government in which the rich would pay all the taxes and the poor would make all the laws. This definition, cynical though it may sound in the second half of the twentieth century, is one reason why democracy is popular with the poor. In the same vein, one may say that the United Nations is popular with the weak, since one purpose of the United Nations is to reduce the role of national power in international relations. It can be argued that the United Nations structure fails to come to grips satisfactorily with the facts of power, that the great powers will not acquiesce in a system in which a great many weak states seek to dispose of the interests of a few strong ones. But one paradox of the present era is that it is no longer possible to guarantee that overwhelming power, in the conventional sense, will secure the goals for which it was created. To put it another way, power is increasingly taking a diversity of forms, and one form of power in the contemporary world is the ability to use the processes of the United Nations to advance national interests.

The countries of the Afro-Asian Group do not possess great military or economic power. The core of most of their economies is subsistence-agriculture; their export trade may be confined to a single product; educational and medical services are inadequate. In some of them, indeed, even the structure of the state is rudimentary. But these countries, conscious of their material weakness, find in the United Nations a forum in which weakness is not a major disadvantage. In the formal sense, the vote of Mauritania counts as much as the vote of the United States.

Within the Afro-Asian Group are a number of sub-alignments. There is an Arab Group, which could be regarded as the UN arm of the League of Arab States. The Arab League has, at one time or another, included Algeria, Iraq, Jordan, Lebanon, Libya, Morocco, Saudi Arabia, Sudan, Syria, Tunisia, the United Arab Republic (Egypt), and Yemen. Major questions of direct concern to the Arab countries are considered by the Council of the Arab League, which meets from time to time in one of the Arab countries. The Arab League has an office in New York, and the Arab Group at the United Nations normally meets at least once a month. The Arab Group has maintained a fair degree of solidarity of voting, in spite of internal stresses. The United Arab Republic (Egypt) has exerted marked leadership within the Group.

The Arab Group has included countries with revolutionary governments (Iraq, the United Arab Republic), as well as more conservative monarchies (Saudi Arabia, Libya), but one political issue unites them: hostility to Israel. Arabs regard the Israelis as intruders who have stolen Arab lands and driven out Arab people. In 1948, the Arabs took up arms against Israel and in 1956 Israel invaded Egypt; on both occasions the United Nations succeeded in bringing the fighting to an end. Israel's Arab neighbours consider themselves at war with Israel. There is a total economic and political boycott, and ships with cargoes destined for Israel have not been allowed through the Suez Canal. One million Arab refugees from Palestine live in the Arab countries and insist that they wish to return to their homes in what was formerly Palestine.

In 1958, following a conference of independent African

states held in Accra, an African Group of nine states came into existence at the United Nations. The number of African members of the United Nations, excluding South Africa, now exceeds thirty. There have been some divisions among African states so that there are now several African associations. There is a radical group associated with the conference of African states held in Casablanca in 1961; it consists of Algeria, Ghana, Guinea, Mali, Morocco and the United Arab Republic. Representatives of most of the former French territories in Africa met in Brazzaville in 1960 and continue to co-operate in UN affairs. The Brazzaville states are: Cameroun, the Central African Republic, Chad, Congo (formerly French, with capital at Brazzaville), Dahomey, Gabon, the Ivory Coast, Madagascar, Mauritania, Niger, Senegal and Upper Volta. The Brazzaville countries took part in the conference which met in Monrovia in 1961; the other states attending the Monrovia conference were: Ethiopia, Liberia, Libya, Nigeria, Sierra Leone, Somalia, Togo and Tunisia.

The Asian member-states, excluding nationalist China and those Asian countries which are usually regarded as part of the Middle East, are twelve in number: Burma, Cambodia, Ceylon, India, Indonesia, Japan, Laos, Malaya, Nepal, Pakistan, the Philippines and Thailand. The two last-named countries belong to SEATO, and Pakistan belongs to both CENTO and SEATO; Japan has military arrangements with the United States. The other countries are generally regarded as neutralist in outlook and, except for Laos and Malaya, attended the conference of neutral nations in Belgrade in 1961.

Perhaps the most interesting group of all is the Commonwealth, since it has neither geographical nor ideological unity. Commonwealth members of the UN are as follows:

Europe	Asia	The Americas	Africa	Oceania
Cyprus*	Ceylon	Canada	Ghana	New Zealand
United Kingdom	India	Jamaica	Nigeria	Australia
	Malaya	Trinidad and Tobago	Sierra Leone	
	Pakistan		Tanganyika	
			Uganda	

* For some UN purposes, Cyprus has been regarded as part of the Middle East.

The Commonwealth Group was once described to me in the following terms: "The Commonwealth cannot be defined, but it undoubtedly exists. We meet from time to time to exchange ideas on matters on which we are agreed. We always vote for each other, unless we happen to prefer some other candidate. It is a very superior form of co-operation but it cannot be copied."

The Commonwealth Group meets about twice a month during sessions of the General Assembly, and irregularly at other times. Proceedings are informal; as there is normally no attempt at reaching an agreed conclusion, voting is not resorted to. Commonwealth countries often agree on candidates for election to Commonwealth seats on UN organs, but this is usually arranged informally rather than at meetings of the group.

The dynamic nature of international politics inevitably leads to changes in the composition and outlook of some of the groups. A localised dispute within a region may be followed by differences on wider issues. In the Arab world and Africa, in particular, alignments are often in a fluid state. Internal differences within a group may manifest themselves in split votes in the General Assembly, but without actually leading to changes of alignment. For many years, for example, Western countries have not agreed about Chinese representation in the United Nations, and this has been reflected in the voting.

Bloc-voting is, perhaps, most interesting where it is least visible—that is to say, in secret balloting. All elections by the General Assembly are by secret ballot, and there are supposed to be no nominations. When the General Assembly comes to elect members of the three Councils or those of its own officers elected by the plenary, there is a theoretically unfettered choice. There is, to be sure, nearly always a general understanding about the distribution or rotation of certain seats, but this cannot prevent two or more candidates from offering themselves for a particular vacancy. And the situation is complicated by the legal requirement of the Charter that a two-thirds majority is needed in some elections. This means that a minority of member-states (one-third plus one) can compel the Assembly to continue balloting indefinitely. In 1959, for example, the General Assembly held more than fifty inconclusive ballots to fill one seat on the Security Council. There were two candidates, Poland and Turkey. So long as each of these states could muster at least twenty-nine votes on every ballot, the other candidate could not secure the two-thirds majority needed for election. In all ballots until the last, Poland's vote never fell below thirty-six and Turkey's never below thirty-three. In the end, a compromise was reached by which the two candidates split the two-year term of office between them.

It is interesting to note, in passing, that difficulties of this sort might be greatly reduced if the Assembly were to establish a nominations committee. The League of Nations, on the suggestion of Norway, decided in 1936 to set up a nominations committee. The creation of a nominations committee was favoured by a majority of members of the United Nations in 1945, but not by the necessary two-thirds majority, and so the matter was dropped. The idea was revived, without success, by Sweden in 1947 and by Canada in 1949.

CHAPTER IV

PEACE-KEEPING

PEACE-KEEPING by the United Nations may involve three different kinds of action: efforts to remove the causes of conflict (*prevention**); attempts to settle by peaceful means those disputes which are not prevented and which endanger world peace (*peaceful settlement*); and coercive measures in the event of an immediate threat to peace or act of aggression (*enforcement*).

The states which are members of the United Nations and the related agencies are committed to a programme of international co-operation "with a view to the creation of conditions of stability and well-being which are necessary for peaceful and friendly relations among nations". This preventive work is most important even though the present scale of it is inadequate.

The third type of action, enforcement, is the responsibility of the Security Council. The Charter lays down a graduated series of enforcement measures which may be taken by the Council; member-states are formally required, by their membership in the United Nations, to join in affording mutual assistance in carrying out such enforcement measures. The measures may be non-military in character (economic sanctions or the severance of diplomatic relations) or they may involve the use of armed force (military demonstrations, blockades, or direct military operations). A member-state which disrupts the peace

* The word *prevention* is here used in the sense of action to forestall or avoid a situation. Preventive action, in the UN Charter, means provisional measures taken by the Security Council to prevent an aggravation of a situation and is without prejudice to the rights, claims, or position of the parties concerned.

may be suspended from the rights of membership or expelled from the United Nations "by the General Assembly upon the recommendation of the Security Council".

Although the Security Council has primary responsibility for maintaining world peace, it can apply enforcement measures or take other substantive action only if the five permanent members are in agreement. A dissenting vote by a permanent member of the Council on a question of substance represents a veto, and the threat or use of the veto has meant that the Security Council has not usually been in a position to authorise enforcement measures.

The United Nations has not, however, been powerless as an instrument of peace-keeping, since there are many techniques short of enforcement which may be used to reduce the dangers. The question of disarmament is dealt with in Chapter V; I consider here some of the peace-keeping techniques which are specified in that part of the Charter concerned with the pacific settlement of disputes. It should be emphasised that many disputes in the nuclear age are never "settled" in any final sense; the world has learned to live with situations which, in earlier ages, might have seemed intolerable. Palestine and Kashmir, for example, have been on the agenda of the Security Council for fifteen years.

The Charter states that the parties to any dispute which is likely to endanger international peace and security "shall, first of all, seek a solution by negotiation, enquiry, mediation, conciliation, arbitration, judicial settlement, resort to regional agencies or arrangements, or other peaceful means of their own choice". It may be as well, at this point, to define the terms used in this part of the Charter.

Direct *negotiation* is a normal diplomatic procedure involving the parties to a dispute. *Enquiry* seeks to establish the facts and a clarification of the issues in order to contribute to a settlement. The use of *good offices* is not specifically mentioned in the Charter, though it is covered by the phrase "other peaceful means". It involves the intervention of a third party in order to bring the parties together, but no proposal is made as to a solution. *Mediation* and *conciliation* also involve third-party intervention, mediation usually being by a single individual, while conciliation is usually by a commission consisting of members nominated by each of the parties and one or more neutral members. A solution may be suggested in mediation and conciliation, though the parties are not bound to accept it. *Arbitration* is a method of settling disputes by reference to a tribunal, usually appointed specially for the purpose by the parties, or by agreement between arbitrators already chosen; an arbitral award is binding on the parties. Arbitration is a form of third-party settlement which is especially useful when political rather than legal issues are involved. *Judicial settlement* is suitable for dealing with the legal aspects of disputes and requires their reference to an impartial tribunal for decision on the basis of pre-established law. *Regional agencies or arrangements* must be "consistent with the Purposes and Principles of the United Nations", and it is stipulated that the Security Council shall at all times be kept fully informed of activities for the maintenance of international peace and security which may be "undertaken or in contemplation" on a regional basis.

The United Nations is not a substitute for traditional diplomacy, but if normal diplomatic methods fail, states are under an obligation to resort to the machinery of the United Nations rather than use force unilaterally.

The United Nations has not in practice been regarded simply as an instrument to use when other methods fail. Indeed, resort to the United Nations is often thought of as a form of political pressure rather than a method of solving a problem, because the airing of a dispute in a UN organ may induce in others a more accommodating attitude. Even an aggrieved party can be persuaded to modify its more extravagant demands. For several years Greece sought to put before the United Nations the case for *Enosis* (the union of Cyprus with Greece). Although the debates showed widespread dissatisfaction with British policy in Cyprus at the time, there was little international support for *Enosis*. The consequent abandonment of the demand for *Enosis* made possible the final compromise solution of an independent Cyprus, with guarantees for the Turkish-speaking minority, which was reached in 1959 between the British, Greek, and Turkish governments.

Two points may be noted about the role of the United Nations regarding Cyprus. First, while consideration of the Cyprus question by the United Nations eventually created a climate of opinion favourable to a solution, the actual agreement was negotiated outside the United Nations by the parties concerned. Secondly, while UN *debates* were clearly influential, and actual *resolutions* were not intrinsically of great importance. The decisions of the General Assembly over a five-year period are shown in Table IV.

TABLE IV

GENERAL ASSEMBLY DECISIONS REGARDING CYPRUS, 1954–58

Session	Decision
1954	Decided not to adopt a resolution.
1955	Rejected Greek request to place the matter on the agenda.
1956/7	Expressed the hope that negotiations would lead to a peaceful, democratic and just solution in accordance with the Charter.
1957	No resolution adopted.
1958	Expressed confidence that continued efforts would be made by the parties to reach a solution in line with the resolution of 1956/7.

Some international crises are caused, in part at least, by genuine misunderstanding by one state of the intentions of another state. In these circumstances, the formal and informal processes of "parliamentary" diplomacy are often sufficient to bring the difficulties to an end. Consider, for example, the now forgotten Middle Eastern crisis of October 1957.

Syria complained to the United Nations that Turkish troops had been concentrated close to the Syrian-Turkish frontier in such a way as to provoke frontier incidents and threaten Syria's security. The Syrian government was obviously alarmed by the situation, fearing that a deterioration might lead to outright hostilities. It became evident during the course of the UN debates and discussions, however, that Turkey's military dispositions were defensive in purpose. International consideration of the question helped to keep tempers in check until it became clear that there was an element of misunderstanding in the whole business. A fortnight after the issue was raised, there was general agreement that the danger was over and that the matter could safely be dropped.

Most international crises, however, arise from a serious conflict of interests rather than from misunderstanding. It would seem to have been the intention of the founders of the United

Nations that major questions affecting world peace would ordinarily go to the Security Council, but increasingly since 1950 such issues have been submitted to the General Assembly. Whichever organ is used, it is first necessary that the parties to the dispute, and others concerned, should present their versions of the facts and of the points at issue. The parties will normally be states, but if one of the parties is not a member of the United Nations, friendly states may in effect act as spokesmen of the absent party. Countries of the Afro-Asian Group acted in this way on behalf of the Algerian nationalists until Algeria became independent in 1962.

After the facts have been established (or even before, if outright hostilities are threatened or in progress), there is often a move to stabilise the situation by provisional measures which are without prejudice to any rights or claims of the parties. Such provisional measures normally involve a call to the parties to cease from actions contrary to the Charter and to settle their differences by peaceful means. If such a call does not prove sufficient, the UN organ concerned may then approve some specific procedure for promoting a solution. If the decision is taken by the General Assembly, it is not legally binding on the parties; decisions of the Security Council, on the other hand, must be accepted and carried out by member-states.

One can illustrate some of the techniques open to the United Nations by reference to some major decisions taken by UN organs regarding Indonesia over a three-year period.* A bare recital of UN decisions does not, of course, give any idea of the amount of unseen diplomatic and related activity undertaken by the UN Secretariat and member-governments in support of the decisions of the political organs.

If a dispute has deteriorated so that actual hostilities have broken out, and the United Nations is eventually successful in arranging a cease-fire, it may be necessary to establish an impartial system of observation to ensure that all parties adhere to the agreement. For this purpose the United Nations can draw on its own small Field Service. After cease-fire

* See Table V, page 58. The choice of the Indonesian question has no particular significance; the Palestine question or Kashmir or the Congo would have served equally well, except that these questions fall within the category of "unfinished business".

TABLE V

SOME MAJOR UN DECISIONS REGARDING INDONESIA, 1947–50

1 August 1947	Security Council calls on the parties (the Netherlands and Indonesia) to cease hostilities forthwith and to settle their disputes by arbitration or by other peaceful means.
25 August 1947	Council establishes commission at Batavia to report on the situation in Indonesia; also establishes committee of good offices to assist in the pacific settlement of the dispute.
26 August 1947	Council calls on the parties to adhere to the recommendation for a cease-fire.
1 November 1947	Council again calls on the parties to give effect to the cease-fire resolution.
28 February 1948	Council welcomes truce agreement reached on 17 January 1948.
29 July 1948	Council calls for strict observance of truce agreement and for full and early implementation of the agreed political principles.
18 December 1948	The Netherlands denounces truce and resumes hostilities.
24 December 1948	Security Council calls for an immediate cessation of hostilities and release of political prisoners.
28 December 1948	Security Council calls upon the Netherlands to release all political prisoners; asks its commission in Indonesia to supply "information and guidance".
28 January 1949	Security Council calls upon the Netherlands to discontinue all military operations and to release political prisoners, calls for negotiations between the parties, and establishes new Commission for Indonesia to assist the parties to implement the resolution.
7 December 1949	General Assembly welcomes the agreement which had been reached between Indonesia and the Netherlands at a round table conference in The Hague.
28 September 1950	Indonesia admitted to the United Nations.

agreements had been reached between Israel and the neighbouring Arab states (1949) and between India and Pakistan in Kashmir (1950), UN observer missions were sent to check on compliance. In both cases personnel of the UN Field Service were supplemented by specially recruited staff. These missions are still at work, at an annual cost to members of the United Nations of more than $2 million.

These "observation" duties should be distinguished from

parallel efforts at mediation or conciliation as well as from operations of the police type. The first large-scale policing operation of the United Nations was initiated after the Anglo-French-Israeli action in Suez in 1956. The situation then required a more substantial form of UN presence than the truce supervision organisation of a few hundred men which was in the Middle East at that time.

The Suez crisis arose simultaneously with the Hungarian crisis, and there were initially a number of points of similarity between the two. Both questions arose first in the Security Council; in both cases action by the Security Council was prevented by the use of the veto; both questions were thereupon transferred to the General Assembly under an emergency procedure; in both cases the Assembly called for a cessation of hostilities and the withdrawal of foreign troops.

But there the similarity ends. The Soviet attitude regarding Hungary never wavered. The Soviet government was not disposed to modify its policy on a question it regarded as vital to its security. Neither Mr. Hammarskjöld nor an observer group nominated by him nor a committee of enquiry established by the General Assembly was permitted to visit Hungary. The Security Council, the General Assembly, and the Secretary-General adhered throughout to certain positions of principle, but this had no discernible effect on the immediate situation.

In the Suez case, two processes were at work. Diplomatic pressure was exerted, both through the United Nations and by other means, for the withdrawal of foreign forces from Egypt. At the same time, the United Nations entered upon a major police action, an experiment for which Dag Hammarskjöld and Lester Pearson (Canada) must share most of the credit. An international emergency force, under a United Nations commander, was inserted between the belligerents. Its primary task was to "secure and supervise the cessation of hostilities" —a phrase more precise about the end to be pursued than about the means to be adopted.

The UN Emergency Force served several purposes. It symbolised the concern of the international community; its presence at the scene of the trouble had a tranquillising effect on the parties; the invaders were enabled to withdraw from an untenable situation; the opposing forces were prevented from assaulting each other without first assaulting the United Nations. The peak complement of the UN Force was 6,000 officers and men loaned by member-states. It was not sent to the Middle East to enforce a solution or to change the military or political situation, and it was instructed to use force only in self-defence.

On the basis of the early experience of this UN Emergency Force, Hammarskjöld outlined certain "basic principles and rules" which he hoped would provide "an adaptable framework for later operations". Among these principles were:

1. The United Nations cannot station units on the territory of a member-state without the consent of the government concerned;
2. It is for the United Nations alone to decide on the composition of any force, taking fully into account the views of the host government;
3. UN forces should not include units from any of the five permanent members of the Security Council or from any country which might be considered as having a special interest in the situation;
4. UN forces should have full freedom of movement and all facilities necessary for their tasks;
5. The personnel of a UN force should be loyal to the aims of the Organisation, and the force should be directly responsible to one of the main organs of the United Nations;
6. United Nations personnel cannot be a party to any internal conflict, and a UN force should not be used to enforce any specific political solution or to influence the political balance;
7. Because a UN force is an instrument for mediation and conciliation, it cannot engage in combat activities, though it may respond with force to an armed attack;
8. The cost should be allocated among member-states according to the normal scale of budgetary contributions.

It is difficult to plan precisely about the composition or operation of United Nations forces. Important precedents were created when the UN Emergency Force was set up in 1956, but when another crisis arose in the Middle East in

1958, a quite different form of UN presence was needed. Lebanon had complained to the United Nations of interference by the United Arab Republic, and the Security Council decided to set up an observation group to prevent illegal infiltration across the Lebanese borders. The observation group in Lebanon was not a "force", even of a police type. At its maximum it consisted of some 600 observers, mainly military officers, drawn from twenty-one countries, and equipped with reconnaissance vehicles and aircraft.

Three months later, when Mr. Hammarskjöld was asked by the General Assembly to make "practical arrangements" to uphold the Charter in Jordan, which had also complained of interference by the United Arab Republic, he did not consider it appropriate to despatch even a border observation group. All that was needed in Jordan was a small diplomatic staff composed of members of the United Nations Secretariat.

Before considering the extent to which the principles derived from the Middle East operations were later found applicable in the Congo, it may be worth contrasting the experience of the UN Emergency Force with the Korean action launched by the United Nations six years earlier. The Korean operation represented collective resistance to aggression, and the United Nations was engaged for three years in severe military action against North Korean and Chinese troops. The United States was placed in charge of a unified command; most of the troops came from the United States, but fifteen other states supplied at least token combat units and five countries provided medical contingents.

Some of the more important differences between the Korean and Suez operations are shown below:

Korea	*Suez*
Authorised by Security Council.	Authorised by General Assembly.
Purpose was to assist a victim of aggression; therefore engaged in combat activity.	Purpose was to secure the cessation of hostilities; force kept to a minimum and used only in self-defence.
Security Council requested the United States to designate the commander.	Commander appointed by the General Assembly, upon the recommendation of the Secretary-General.

Korea	*Suez*
Included troops of three of the permanent members of the Security Council.	Troops of permanent members of the Security Council excluded.
Expenses met by governments contributing troops.	Expenses allocated among all UN members on ordinary budget scale (although not all have paid).

The Congo operation, which began in 1960, shared one characteristic with other UN operations—its uniqueness. In some respects it was akin to the UN action in Lebanon in 1958 in that conditions of virtual civil war prevailed at times and that one task of the United Nations was to prevent illegal infiltration from outside. But the scale was entirely different; the observation group in Lebanon had consisted of a few hundred men whereas the Congo Force numbered 20,000 at its peak. Of the principles derived from the Suez experience (see page 60), numbers 1, 2, 4, 5, and 8 were applicable in the Congo. Hammarskjöld again excluded from the Force units from permanent members of the Security Council, but he did not adhere to his earlier position regarding the use of contingents from states with a special interest in the situation. The Congo Force was, to the greatest extent possible, drawn from African countries, though with important additions from Asia, Canada, Ireland, and Sweden.

United Nations personnel in the Congo were, as a matter of course, instructed at the start to avoid involvement in internal Congolese politics (principle 6), but the decision to maintain the unity of the Congo in the face of separatist activities eventually required UN officials to take action which had, or could be interpreted as having, internal political implications. While the United Nations exercised restraint in using force (principle 7), the Security Council did in the end authorise the use of force if necessary, as a last resort, for certain limited and defined purposes.

The principle that the cost of peace-keeping operations should be allocated among member-states according to the normal scale of budgetary assessments, which had been approved by the General Assembly, was maintained in theory only, both for the Middle East and the Congo. At the end of 1962, seventy-one member-states were in arrears for peace-

keeping operations, the total amount owing to the United
Nations being $104 million. The Soviet republics were $54
million in arrears, and the other Warsaw Pact countries owed
$9 million. France owed $14 million for the Congo and Belgium had accumulated arrears of $3 million. Nationalist China
owed $10 million and South Africa $1 million. All the Latin
American states were in arrears; so were all the Arab states.

The non-payers have used legal and political arguments.
From the legal point of view, they have said that the costs of
peace-keeping operations are not "expenses of the Organisation" which, according to the Charter, are apportioned among
member-states as decided by the General Assembly. Their
political case is simply that the states which caused the trouble
should meet the cost of clearing up the mess.

The refusal of states to pay the cost of peace-keeping operations threatened to bring the United Nations to the verge of
bankruptcy. Two actions were decided upon in 1961 in an effort
to stave off financial disaster. First, the General Assembly
authorised U Thant to issue United Nations bonds to the
equivalent of $200 million and to include in the regular budget
an amount to pay interest charges on such bonds at 2 per cent
per annum and to cover any instalments of principal due. By
the end of 1962, fifty-three member-states had announced
their intention of purchasing bonds, to a total amount of $121
million, of which bonds to the value of $108 million had
actually been purchased; in addition, five non-members had
purchased bonds to the value of £13 million.*

The second action taken in 1961 was to request the International Court of Justice to advise whether the expenses of
peace-keeping operations in the Middle East and the Congo
are "expenses of the Organisation" within the meaning of the
Charter. The Court's advisory opinion on this point was of
great importance for the future of the United Nations.

The Court recognised that any interpretation of the UN
Charter was likely to have political significance. At the same
time, the Court considered that it had been invited to undertake
an essentially judicial task, and it was not able to attribute a
political motive to the Assembly's request. The Court had been
asked to give an advisory opinion upon a concrete legal question.

* These non-members were: German Federal Republic, Republic
of Korea (South), Kuwait, Switzerland and Viet-Nam (South).

The Court rejected the contention that the Charter implied the qualifying adjective "regular" or "administrative" before the references to budget and expenses, and it considered that the practice of the Organisation had been entirely consistent with the plain meaning of the text.

It had been argued before the Court that expenses resulting from operations for maintaining international peace and security are not "expenses of the Organisation". The argument rested in part upon the view that, when the maintenance of peace and security is involved, only the Security Council can authorise action. The Court pointed out that the Security Council has primary authority for maintaining peace and security, and only the Security Council can require enforcement by coercive action against an aggressor. But the Security Council's responsibility is not exclusive, and the Charter makes it abundantly clear that the General Assembly is also to be concerned with international peace and security. The provisions of the Charter which distribute functions and powers to the Security Council and the General Assembly do not exclude from the General Assembly the power to provide for the financing of measures designed to maintain peace and security, and the Court could find no basis for limiting the budgetary authority of the General Assembly in this respect. Whenever the United Nations takes action to fulfil one of its stated purposes, the expenses incurred are "expenses of the Organisation", even if the action should have been taken by the wrong organ.

The operations in the Middle East and the Congo were undertaken to fulfil a prime purpose of the United Nations, that is to say, to promote and maintain peace, though they were not enforcement actions.

The Court was of the opinion, by nine votes to five, that the expenditures incurred are "expenses of the Organisation", and the General Assembly accepted the advisory opinion. The General Assembly set up a working party to study "the situation arising from the arrears of some member-states" as well as "special methods for financing peace-keeping operations". A special session of the General Assembly is to meet before the end of June 1963 in order to consider further the financial situation of the Organisation.

For the foreseeable future there will inevitably be an element of improvisation in UN policing and similar peace-keeping operations. Important political, legal, and financial issues are at stake, but certain technical steps could be taken to prepare for future emergencies. A small planning staff in the UN Secretariat could, on the basis of past experience, make advance preparations for various types of operation. Member-states could earmark personnel and give them the special police-type training needed for UN police duties; they could also earmark transport aircraft for moving contingents for the United Nations at short notice.

If this were a book about the United Nations as I would like the Organisation to be rather than the United Nations as it is, I would give more prominent attention to judicial methods of dealing with the legal aspects of international disputes. Respect for law is, after all, a mark of civilisation. Within a democratic nation, any threat to the legal order or dispute about a legal question is dealt with by impartially administered judicial process.

If nations are to live in peace, their relations must to some extent be governed by legal rules and principles. It must be admitted, however, that international law is at present rudimentary. It is largely uncodified, and the means for enforcing international legal decisions are inadequate.

Two UN organs are exclusively concerned with international law. The International Court of Justice, with its seat at The Hague, is the principal judicial organ of the United Nations. It decides those disputes between states which are submitted to it, and gives advisory opinions on legal questions. The International Law Commission, a subsidiary organ of the General Assembly, has no responsibility for adjudication but is charged with promoting the progressive development and codification of international law.

All members of the United Nations are automatically parties to the Statute of the International Court of Justice; some states which do not belong to the United Nations have become parties to the Statute.* Each member of the United Nations has expressly undertaken to comply with the decision of the Court in any case to which it is a party.

A state may opt to accept the compulsory jurisdiction of the Court, either unconditionally or on condition of reciprocity or

* See Appendix II, page 128.

for a certain time, but fewer than half the parties to the Statute have exercised this option. The United States and a few other countries have accepted compulsory jurisdiction but have excluded all disputes with regard to matters which are essentially of domestic jurisdiction (which are, in any event, outside the competence of the Court); and have further provided that the state concerned rather than the Court shall determine whether the matter is domestic or not. The basis for this reservation in the United States is a resolution of the Senate of 2 August 1946—the so-called Connally Amendment.

There have always been those who have regarded international law as the heart of the problem of international relations. The progressive achievement of order and peace within states has been accompanied by increasing respect for law and legal institutions. But we live in a highly political age. Marxists regard law as being a reflection of social relations and material conditions. Many leaders of the newer countries of Asia and Africa are distrustful of aspects of international law which seem to inhibit change. The Rule of Law brings many blessings, but it is not synonymous with absolute justice —whatever that may be.

The International Court has given some important decisions and advisory opinions, but more use could be made of it in dealing with legal aspects of international disputes. Unlike national courts, the International Court cannot exercise jurisdiction unless the parties agree; the direction in which to move is to extend the area of compulsory jurisdiction. There is, in almost every international dispute, some element susceptible of judicial solution. There would be much to be said for including in future international agreements an undertaking by the parties to accept the jurisdiction of the Court over any legal differences that might arise.

The other legal organ of the United Nations, the International Law Commission, has made a little progress in codifying international law; that is to say, in drafting international legal instruments on subjects on which there is already a fair measure of agreement. It has registered notable success in the field of Diplomatic Relations, and limited success regarding the Law of the Sea. The Commission has hardly come to grips yet with its other task of "developing" international law.

The danger of the present situation is that states are reluctant to use judicial methods of settling disputes, and yet the political alternatives are unsatisfactory. The Security Council can be blocked by great power veto, and to transfer the issue to the General Assembly does not eliminate the power realities which the veto symbolises. The General Assembly is an unwieldy organ, and most of its decisions are only recommendations or expressions of opinion. Like any deliberative body, it is sometimes preoccupied with trivialities while important tasks are neglected.

Even if the policy-making organs fail to act effectively, the responsibilities of the Secretary-General and staff continue. Indeed, during Hammarskjöld's tenure of office, the role of the Secretariat, and particularly of the Secretary-General, assumed great importance in the political field. When policy-making organs failed to agree, it was tempting to "leave it to Dag". Time and again Hammarskjöld was entrusted with vital peace-making or peace-keeping responsibilities, although often without being given the resources in money and men or the diplomatic backing which he was entitled to expect. Moreover, Hammarskjöld took a broad view of his responsibilities and did not hesitate to undertake independent initiatives within the framework of the Charter.

The adoption of a resolution by a policy-making organ normally marks the end of a phase, but for the Secretariat it is almost always the beginning of a new phase. In the economic and social field there has developed a close link between research and analysis on the one hand and field-operations on the other, but this has been less true in the political field. Efforts to develop systematic techniques for dealing with political crises have been made from time to time, but with only limited success. The United Nations nearly always rises to the occasion if there is a real crisis, but it often gives the impression of improvising.

The "peace" which the United Nations seeks to maintain is precarious. Indeed, it is one of the paradoxes of the UN system that one way of getting international attention is to endanger world peace. While it is no doubt an exaggeration to assert, as did one United Nations delegate, that the United Nations Charter is "a standing invitation to violence", the fact remains that discontent sometimes becomes a matter of international concern only when it erupts into violence.

CHAPTER V

DISARMAMENT

THE word *disarmament* has a high emotional content. To some people it signifies the state of military unpreparedness which characterised the European democracies during the time when Hitler's Germany was growing in strength, an unpatriotic attitude of appeasement and moral surrender, an attempt to substitute slogans for the realities of power. Others think of disarmament as a simple cure for all international ills, a cure which is beyond man's reach only because of the selfishness or stupidity of a few diplomats, soldiers, scientists, or businessmen.

The kind of disarmament which has been considered by UN organs, and with which I am concerned in this chapter, would not require that any state or group of states should be placed in a position of weakness while other states remain strong. International disarmament would certainly involve risks, but so does international rearmament; there is no policy without risk.

But equally it should be emphasised that the case for disarmament is damaged if too many things, or the wrong things, are claimed for it. All disarmament-measures do not necessarily reduce international tension; unilateral disarmament by one state or by a group of states could have important moral or political consequences, but there can be no guarantee that the example would be copied by others. An international agreement on disarmament is certainly no panacea. It is a course of action designed to diminish specific dangers. The purpose of international disarmament is to reduce the particular risks which arise from the existence and nature of weapons and not, directly, the risks arising from the political and other conditions which lead nations to make military preparations.

A great danger in the nuclear age is war by accident, misunderstanding, or miscalculation. The nuclear powers have no doubt taken elaborate precautions to prevent the *accidental* detonation of nuclear devices. It is possible to take steps to reduce, though not to eliminate, the danger of war by *misunderstanding*: the possibility that preparations by nation *A* for defence or retaliation might be thought by nation *B* to be of aggressive intent, leading to a pre-emptive strike by nation *B* against nation *A*. But it is impossible to eliminate entirely the risk of *miscalculation*. The doctrine of the deterrent, or any alternative military doctrine, must assume that nations are more likely to act rationally than irrationally, although our knowledge of human beings convinces us that they do not always do so.

The risk of war by accident, misunderstanding or miscalculation has always existed. Indeed, there is a sense in which just about every war in modern times arose from one or other of these circumstances. In pre-nuclear times, however, it was at least theoretically possible to go into reverse in the event of war by mistake, or to win such a war, or to lose but live to fight another day. But modern weapons are delivered so fast and with such accuracy, and are so destructive in their effects, that it is no longer reasonable to rely on these possibilities. There is a point beyond which nuclear weapons, once the decision to launch them has been taken, cannot be recalled; and there would be no victor in any intelligible sense in an all-out nuclear war.

Moreover, every war between nuclear powers would be potentially a nuclear war, and the risks increase as nuclear weapons are more widely disseminated.

The nuclear deterrent is not a means of resisting aggression; it is an attempt to prevent aggression from taking place by threatening to retaliate if it does, on a massive scale if necessary. The threat of nuclear retaliation will not deter if it is not "credible". This does not mean that the exercise of massive retaliation in case of provocation must be absolutely certain, only that there must be enough risk of its being exercised to make it unwise to provoke it. The actual use of the nuclear deterrent would obviously be an admission that it had failed;

and it would doubtless provoke counter-retaliation. The doctrine of the nuclear deterrent requires that, as a last resort, all-out nuclear war should be acceptable to public opinion, that is to say, preferable in certain circumstances to any conceivable alternative.

The nature of the nuclear dilemma has driven men to hope that war can be limited. Unlimited war, it is argued, is suicidal; surrender is unthinkable; therefore it is in everyone's interests to agree in advance to limit future wars.

There are several varieties of the theory of limited war. One school of thought would regard wars fought for certain purposes as permissible and other kinds as impermissible. Others would favour prohibiting the use of the more destructive weapons, considering the use of them as too barbarous for civilised nations. Others, again, would ban the use of weapons for certain purposes, such as to terrorise non-combatants. The doctrine of the just war, which is held by many Christians, requires that wars should be fought only if the purpose is righteous, and that the means used should not be excessive.

Unilateral restraint in the conduct of war may be necessary on moral or practical grounds, but there can be no guarantee that it would be reciprocated. War is not a game in which opponents chivalrously and rationally co-operate to see who can win according to agreed rules. If ever nations were to become sufficiently rational to agree to limit war, they would probably find that they could agree to abolish it. In the meantime, we cannot be sure that limited wars would not escalate.

The problem would be much more simple if all aggressive forms of military power ("first strike" weapons) could be totally eliminated at one stroke, leaving states only with retaliatory ("second strike") and defensive weapons. Unfortunately, military technologists have developed versatile weapons-systems. Whether a long-range missile with a nuclear war-head is "first strike" or "second strike" would depend on the circumstances in which it was used.

Weapons are a symptom of mistrust. Once the mistrust is removed, the weapons become unnecessary. But negotiations for an international agreement on disarmament proceed on the assumption that arms should be regulated or reduced or even eliminated while mistrust continues. Disarmament in this context thus requires some method or combination of methods for giving confidence that international obligations are honoured. In a world of fallible human beings, such methods of control can never provide a completely foolproof guarantee. All they can do is to make cheating as risky as possible. Even with the best detection system, there will always remain a theoretical possibility that one party to an agreement on disarmament could cheat to a small extent and get away with it. Governments must ask not only whether cheating is theoretically possible but also whether, in any particular set of circumstances, the risks of cheating are greater or less than the risks of not entering into a disarmament-agreement.

Nations rely on different manifestations of military power: so-called conventional (that is to say, pre-nuclear) weapons; nuclear weapons, delivered by manned aircraft or by missile; and less tangible military assets such as morale, geography, and secrecy. There has been research in some countries regarding the use of chemical, biological, and radiological devices for both offensive and defensive purposes. A programme for disarmament, if it is to have any chance of acceptance, must link together various types of military power so that at no stage is any state or group of states in a position of military advantage or disadvantage as a result of disarming.

The long-term aim of disarmament is to eliminate all means of waging war, leaving states with only those forces needed for internal security and for an international force for peace-keeping operations under the United Nations. Opinions differ on whether such an aim could be achieved in a few years or whether it would take decades; but whatever view is taken about duration, a disarmament-programme would have to be carried out in stages, with time-limits for each stage.

There has been a great deal of talk about disarmament in UN organs, but no agreed disarmament. This is not because nations are cynical or hypocritical. The problem is complex, there are risks in disarming as well as in not disarming, and there are doubtless minority groups in all countries with a vested interest in maintaining or expanding military establishments.

There have been four main phases in UN activities in the field of disarmament. During the *first phase*, from 1946 to 1954, relatively unproductive debates on disarmament took place in various UN organs consisting of the members of the Security Council, plus Canada when nuclear questions were involved.

In 1954, however, a *second phase* began which was more fruitful. In April of that year, there was created a negotiating sub-committee consisting of the Soviet Union, the United States, Britain, France, and Canada. In this more intimate setting, it became possible to have an exchange of views on a more realistic basis. On 11 June 1954, Britain and France presented a proposal for an immediate ban on the use of nuclear weapons except in defence against aggression, and a phased programme of disarmament, linking conventional and nuclear weapons, with appropriate control-measures. The Soviet Union rejected the Anglo-French plan when it was first presented, but agreed the following September that it should form the basis for future negotiations.

These negotiations took place in 1955–7 and resulted in a considerable narrowing of the gap between the two sides. At first major attention was given to the possibility of a balanced and far-reaching programme of general disarmament, but later the emphasis switched to measures of partial disarmament. The Soviet Union, during this period, moved some way to accepting important elements of the Western position. By the time the Soviet Union withdrew from the negotiations in 1957, the following points had been agreed between the two sides.

1. The goal should be disarmament by all states down to the levels needed for maintaining internal security.
2. As a first step towards that goal, and with a view to improving international relations, agreements on partial disarmament should be concluded.
3. There should be no political preconditions to the entry into force of a disarmament-agreement.
4. International disarmament should proceed by stages.
5. Conventional disarmament should begin with reductions in armed forces and weapons. For the first stage there should be ceilings of 2·5 million men for the United States and the Soviet Union, and 750,000 for Britain and France. For the second stage the ceilings should be 2·1 million and 700,000, and for the third stage 1·7 million and 650,000.

6. Levels of armed forces at each stage should be "balanced", and each step in the process of disarmament should be designed to increase the security of all.

7. A control-organ should be set up appropriate to the disarmament-measures to be undertaken; it should operate under the aegis of the Security Council.

8. The inspection-system should be as effective as possible and should include reciprocal aerial inspection at some stage.

9. The testing of nuclear weapons should be suspended and controlled.

10. The diversion of nuclear materials to peaceful purposes should begin as soon as possible.

11. The elimination of stocks of nuclear and other weapons by international agreement presents special difficulties because there is no method known to science for detecting concealed stocks.

12. Rockets and outer space objects should be used for peaceful purposes only.

13. Part or all of the savings from internationally supervised disarmament should be used to help the people of the less developed areas.

14. An agreement on disarmament should initially include the big powers and should be implemented within the framework of the United Nations.

The agreement on these points represented a significant achievement, though substantial areas of disagreement remained. Disarmament was, however, taken increasingly seriously by the major governments. The military strength of the two sides was more evenly balanced, and there had been a general "thaw" in international relations.

The Soviet withdrawal from the negotiations in 1957 was followed by a *third phase* which proved barren. During this period, the emphasis was on a piecemeal approach to the problem, and the only issue on which there seemed to be significant progress was that of banning nuclear tests. In the early discussions on disarmament, when the atomic bomb was a United States monopoly, the Soviet Union had urged the immediate prohibition of nuclear weapons. The West, alarmed at the size of Soviet conventional forces, was unwilling to renounce its nuclear capacity without some corresponding Soviet step. There was, however, increasing anxiety about the dangers from radioactive fall-out caused by the testing of nuclear weapons. In 1958 a UN scientific committee reported that even the smallest amounts of radiation, whether from fall-out or otherwise, are liable to cause harmful effects. Ten days later, a conference of experts from countries of both Eastern and Western blocs reported that it was technically feasible to set up a workable and effective system for the detection of violations of an agreement on the cessation of nuclear weapons tests. It was recommended that such an international control-system should comprise a network of 160–170 land-based posts and about ten ships, each staffed by about thirty persons. If the control-posts should detect an event which could be suspected of being a nuclear explosion, the international control-organ should send a suitably equipped inspection-group to the site of the event in order to determine whether or not a nuclear explosion had taken place.

This was the setting for the informal moratorium on testing and the three-power negotiations for a formal treaty. Each of the three nuclear powers (the Soviet Union, the United States, and Britain) announced in 1958, in its own terms, the conditions on which it would refrain from testing; France, which was not then a nuclear power, did not consider itself bound by this tacit understanding.

There were several reasons why nuclear tests were isolated for separate consideration. First, nuclear weapons have harmful effects not only when used but also when tested, and these effects are not confined to the testing country. Secondly, a ban on testing would be relatively simple to control. Thirdly, a test ban agreement would hinder the development of independent nuclear weapons programmes by *"Nth"* countries. Fourthly, nuclear weapons had, for millions of people, become a symbol of the arms-race; here was a test of the good intentions of the major powers.

The negotiations on nuclear tests were, in the main, conducted in a serious atmosphere and there was considerable progress in drafting a formal treaty. In the spring of 1961, however, the Soviet government introduced a new issue into the negotiations by insisting that the *troika* principle should apply to the administration of the control-agency. Later in the year, the Soviet government announced that it was resuming tests, and the first Soviet test took place the next day. The West was unprepared for an immediate resumption of atmospheric testing, but underground tests by the United States were resumed after a few weeks and atmospheric tests some months later.

It was assumed, before the *troika* question was raised in the context of nuclear tests, that the main points at issue between the Soviet Union and the two Western powers were as follow:

1. The size of the annual quota of veto-free on-the-spot inspections needed to ensure that detected but unidentified events are earthquakes and not underground nuclear explosions;
2. The exact period of a moratorium over small underground explosions, pending joint research on improving inspection-techniques, and the nature of such research;
3. The phasing of the installation of the control-system;
4. The extent to which the staff of control-posts and inspection-teams should be drawn from the host country.

International pressure to end nuclear tests continued throughout the period of testing in 1961–2, and the General Assembly urged in 1962 that tests should cease not later than 1 January 1963. The General Assembly asked for the conclusion of a treaty prohibiting nuclear tests in all environments for all time, with effective and prompt international verification, and gave its blessing to a compromise proposal on inspection which had been made by eight of the nations participating in the Geneva negotiations.

During the closing weeks of 1962, attention was being directed to a proposal for unmanned inspection-posts; this had been recommended by a number of Soviet and US scientists at an unofficial conference earlier in the year (the "Pugwash conference"). The proposal had been designed to meet the Western demand for international seismic stations with obligatory on-site inspection of suspicious events by an international commission, as well as the Soviet wish to limit on-site inspection because of the fear that it might be a cover for espionage.

The proposal for unmanned stations, or "black boxes" as

they were called, envisaged that they would be self-contained, and sealed in such a way that they could not be tampered with. The instruments would be installed by the host government and periodically returned to the international control-commission. All the records from the instruments would be turned over to the international commission, which would have the right at any time to request the immediate return of the sealed instruments as well as other relevant seismic data. The scientists thought that a system developed along these lines might provide a large enough mass of objective data so that very few on-site inspections would be needed.

There was, at the end of 1962, some hope that agreement might be in sight. It was assumed that the three nuclear powers had completed the tests for which they had prepared earlier. If the Soviet Union were to agree to exclude underground tests from the scope of a treaty, it was thought that agreement could quickly be reached. If, on the other hand, the Soviet Union were to maintain its position that tests in all environments should be banned, there would be negotiations regarding the maximum number of on-site inspections each year, the number and location of manned control-posts and automatic seismic stations, and the composition of inspection-teams. While a ban on testing nuclear weapons would not be actual disarmament, it would be a measure of arms-control. A test ban, even if the inspection-system were of a limited nature, would provide useful experience for dealing with the much less tractable problems which would be encountered in verifying general and complete disarmament; the psychological and political consequences of success would be very great indeed.

There were various abortive attempts to get to grips with other disarmament questions during the period 1958–61. A new committee on disarmament of twenty-five members was set up by the General Assembly in 1957, but the Soviet Union declared that its composition was unacceptable and refused to take part in its work; the committee never met. In 1958 a conference of experts from East and West met to study measures to guard against surprise-attack. The communist side regarded the problem as essentially political in character, while the West placed the emphasis on technical aspects; the conference suspended its work after six weeks, with no significant progress to report. In 1958 the General Assembly agreed to a Soviet proposal for a commission on disarmament consisting of all UN members, and also appointed a separate committee on the peaceful uses of outer space. The Disarmament Commission held a single and formal meeting; the committee on outer space was boycotted by the Soviet bloc as well as by India and the United Arab Republic.

In 1959, the General Assembly called for a renewal of negotiations on disarmament, urged the nuclear powers to prevent the wider dissemination of nuclear weapons, and set up a new committee on outer space in a form more acceptable to the Soviet bloc. A conference on disarmament, consisting of five NATO countries and five Warsaw Pact countries, met in Geneva some months later, but the negotiations were abruptly terminated by the withdrawal of the communist states; the committee on outer space did not even meet. During its 1960 session the General Assembly again called on the nuclear powers to refrain from relinquishing control of nuclear weapons and upon non-nuclear powers to refrain from making or acquiring them. There were, however, no multilateral negotiations on disarmament in 1961, and the committee on outer space met only to elect officers and then adjourned *sine die*.

This is a dismal catalogue of frustration and failure, but fortunately 1961 represented the end of a chapter and not the end of the story. During the summer of 1961, bilateral discussions between the United States and the Soviet Union led to an important agreement on principles for "general and complete" disarmament (the McCloy-Zorin agreement). This agreement initiated the *fourth phase* in negotiations on disarmament. During the session of the General Assembly later in the year, agreement was reached on the composition of a new negotiating body for disarmament. This was to consist of the Soviet Union and four allies from the Warsaw Pact, five NATO countries (the United States, Britain, France, Italy and Canada), and eight "neutrals" (Brazil, Burma, Ethiopia, India, Mexico, Nigeria, Sweden and the United Arab Republic). This body was known as the Eighteen-Nation Committee on Disarmament, though only seventeen nations took part; France declined to participate in the negotiations. The People's Republic of China was not invited.

The negotiations began in the UN building in Geneva in 1962, and the conference was serviced by United Nations staff. All parties to the Geneva negotiations agreed in principle that the aim should be "general and complete" disarmament; that is to say, that all forms of national military power should be eliminated. The Soviet Union and the United States both presented proposals for disarmament in three stages, and there were parallel negotiations on other measures for disarmament and arms-control, as well as three-power discussions on nuclear tests. In addition to these efforts, the UN committee on the peaceful uses of outer space got down to some serious work.

National proposals on disarmament are no doubt logical and complete when first drafted in foreign ministries, but they rarely see the light of day in their initial forms. As consultation with other departments of government takes place, the proposals undergo revision; the specific becomes vague, ambiguities appear, important ideas are lost. The resulting compromise must then be discussed with allied and friendly governments. A collection of national compromises eventually becomes an allied compromise, in which there are new imprecisions. This allied compromise then meets a compromise from the other side, and negotiations take place looking towards an international compromise.

If the matter is seen in this light, it should be emphasised that there were substantial elements of common ground in the plans for general and complete disarmament which were presented by the Soviet Union and the United States in 1962. On the surface at any rate, the two sides agreed about a lot and disagreed about a little. On the other hand, the points of disagreement between the two sides, though no doubt small when compared with what was agreed, were large when attention was directed to the difficulty of bridging the gulf.

Because weapons-technology advances so fast and political conditions are in a state of constant flux, the nature of the problem of disarmament is continually changing. Adjustments in the detailed proposals of the two sides are therefore to be expected. Any statement of positions will no doubt soon be overtaken by new developments, but Table VI summarises some of the differences on disarmament when the Geneva negotiations were adjourned in December 1962.

TABLE VI

MAJOR DIFFERENCES ON DISARMAMENT
(DECEMBER 1962)

	Soviet position	*US position*
1. Duration of disarmament programme	Five years	About nine years
2. Transition from stage to stage	Should be automatic	Should depend on satisfactory completion of previous stage
3. Means of delivery of strategic nuclear weapons	Eliminate in first stage, except for a limited number of missiles to be held by the Soviet Union and the United States in their own territory and eliminated in the second stage	Reduce progressively as part of disarmament process
4. Foreign bases	Eliminate in first stage	Reduce progressively as part of disarmament process, including specified reductions in second stage
5. Inspection	Check that agreed reductions are carried out in each stage (i.e., inspect destruction of arms)	Check that arms retained after each stage are as agreed (i.e., inspect "remainders" of arms)
6. Peace-keeping machinery	National military contingents available on call to UN	International peace force under auspices of UN

I doubt whether the differences relating to the *duration* of a disarmament-programme and transition from stage to stage would prove serious if other differences could be cleared up. The Soviet position on duration makes some appeal to those who wish to see an early end to the arms-race; moreover, it would be easier for states with centrally planned economies to make the drastic changes that would be required by general and complete disarmament than it would be for states with free-enterprise economies. On the other hand, it is clear that total multilateral disarmament, with effective inspection, would be a highly complex process, and it would be to nobody's advantage for the programme to break down because it was being pressed too rapidly.

As for the problem of *transition*, there is something to be said for specifying a realistic timetable in advance. But

whatever initial commitments are undertaken, it is inconceivable that states would proceed from one stage of disarmament
to the next if there were clear evidence that other parties to the
agreement had not completed their obligations under the pre-
vious stage. Indeed, an implicit inducement of self-interest to
honour disarmament-obligations would be the knowledge that
a breakdown, for whatever cause, would lead once again to
all the risks of an uncontrolled arms-race.

The difference between the Soviet Union and the United
States on the timing of the elimination of the *means of
delivery of strategic nuclear weapons* (long-range aircraft and
missiles) was an important one. The Soviet position had been
that the greatest threats to peace should be eliminated in the
first stage. The US view, on the other hand, had been that,
logically, particular types of weapon should disappear as part
of the general process of disarmament. The United States
had also held that retaliatory weapons, far from being a threat
to world peace, had deterred rash military adventures and
aggression, and that to give them up in the first stage of disarmament might have such a destabilising effect as to under-
mine a programme of disarmament.

In September 1962, the Soviet Union went part of the way
towards meeting the US position on means of delivery by sug-
gesting that the two major powers should retain in their own
territory a limited number of missiles until the second stage of
a disarmament-programme. There was a school of thought in
the West which in any case, and independently of disarmament, favoured very substantial reductions in strategic
weapons, if necessary unilaterally by the West alone. This
"minimum deterrent" doctrine held that the super powers
should retain invulnerable or mobile means of delivering a
limited number of strategic nuclear weapons for retaliation on
enemy cities in the event of aggression, but not the much
larger numbers which would be needed for attacking the
enemy's system of nuclear delivery.

The question of *foreign bases* came into sharper focus as a
result of the Cuban affair in 1962; other disarmament-issues
raised by these events were the possibility of establishing
nuclear-free zones and the need to prevent the wider dissemination of nuclear weapons. As regards foreign bases, the
United States position had been that the Soviet proposal to

eliminate foreign bases completely during the first stage of disarmament would place the West in a disadvantageous position; the United States held that foreign bases should disappear gradually as part of the process of disarmament. The McCloy-Zorin agreement had recorded the acceptance by the United States and the Soviet Union of the principle that all disarmament measures should be balanced so that at no stage could any state or group of states gain military advantage as a result of disarmament. One way of resolving the difference between the two sides on this question, in accordance with the McCloy-Zorin principles, would be to link the question of foreign bases with some other disarmament-measure, such as reductions of medium-range missiles or conventional forces. The idea would be that each side should reduce by an agreed amount during the first stage those forms of military power which the other side regards as most provocative.

The differences between the two sides on *inspection* have been of basic importance. The Soviet position has been that the inspectorate should witness the destruction of arms. If two countries had one hundred submarines each and agreed to reduce the number in the first stage of disarmament to sixty each, all that would be necessary—according to this view—would be to ensure that forty were destroyed by each country. The West has maintained that this would make sense only if there were an absolute assurance that the two countries actually had one hundred submarines each to begin with. If one country declared that it began with one hundred when in fact it had one hundred-and-thirty, the destruction of forty by the two countries would leave it with ninety to the other country's sixty. Further stages of disarmament would increase the advantage of concealment. The only way round this difficulty, in the Western view, would be to check that sixty submarines remained in each country at the end of the first stage, not that forty had been destroyed.

This problem symbolises the difference in attitude between the West and the Soviet bloc on the question of inspection. It has sometimes been said that the Soviet Union has wanted disarmament without control and that the West has wanted control without disarmament. The need to link the two processes led M. Moch of France to advance the slogan: "No control without disarmament; no disarmament without control;

but as much disarmament as can be effectively controlled."

Be that as it may, the Soviet Union has given the impression that it accepts the necessity for effective inspection with great reluctance. Secrecy is an important military asset, and because of the nature of Soviet society, it is a more valuable asset to the Soviet Union than it is to the West. If the Soviet bloc is to retain this military advantage, it must press for a form of inspection which would not permit hostile states to use inspection as a means of acquiring significant information about those military dispositions not covered by the agreement. At the same time, there is an inescapable logic in the Western view that the only way to be reasonably certain that both sides are honouring their obligations is to check "remainders".

In order to meet the Soviet anxiety about the possibility that inspection might be improperly used, the United States has made certain proposals for inspection by zonal sampling (the so-called Sohn zones). According to this idea, countries would be divided into regions of roughly equal size and military significance, and governments would deposit with an international agency a sealed declaration of the military installations in each area. A selected region in each country would then be subjected to international inspection; if what was found by the inspectors tallied with what had been declared, another zone in each country would be similarly inspected. The process would follow a fixed timetable related to the stages of a disarmament-agreement. An arrangement of this kind would minimise the extent, but not the effectiveness, of inspection in the early stages; each time the inspectors confirmed that the initial declaration regarding a zone had been accurate, confidence in the good faith of the government concerned would increase.

Inspection by zonal sampling should be distinguished from the various proposals for regional disarmament or arms-control. Inspection by zonal sampling is based on techniques which are commonly used for civilian purposes, and has been put forward as a control-method for general or partial disarmament in a large geographical area. Regional schemes, by contrast, are based on the idea that disarmament, whether partial or total, should begin at points of special danger and insecurity, such as Central Europe where the two sides confront each other directly. Such schemes usually envisage the progressive withdrawal or reduction of forces (*disengagement*) or the banning of certain types of weapons, with appropriate inspection. There is no reason why inspection by zonal sampling should not be combined with a regional scheme of disarmament or arms-control.

Perhaps the most difficult question of all is to plan for a world in which virtually all forms of national military power have been eliminated. This goal, after all, is part of the McCloy-Zorin agreement and has been approved by a unanimous vote of the UN General Assembly. What would be the effect of complete disarmament on international relations? Can total disarmament be reconciled with the idea of national sovereignty? How would international disputes be resolved when nations could no longer use force? What would be the role of the United Nations and the International Court of Justice in a disarmed world?

The McCloy-Zorin agreement states that progress in disarmament should be accompanied by measures to strengthen institutions for maintaining peace and the settlement of international disputes by peaceful means. In the Geneva negotiations, the Soviet Union has urged that these questions be postponed until some progress on disarmament has been achieved. The Soviet Union has, moreover, taken the general position that existing international institutions would be adequate to deal with any problems which might arise in a disarmed world.

The United States has favoured concurrent discussion of disarmament and peace-keeping machinery. It is widely believed in the West not only that there would be many new problems in a disarmed world, but also that nations will not give up significant amounts of military power until they are assured that adequate peace-keeping institutions are being established. The problem is that such institutions necessarily depend on at least limited agreement among the great powers.

Here is the vicious circle. Should nations seek agreement on disarmament in order to reduce international tension, or should they seek to reduce international tension in order to facilitate agreement on disarmament?

CHAPTER VI

DECOLONISATION

Colony is derived from a Latin word meaning "to cultivate", and in its original form referred to people rather than to the land on which they settled. This use of the word is retained in such expressions as "a nudist colony", "the Greek colony in London", "a colony of ants". In the contemporary world, however, a colony is usually thought of as territory in which foreigners have settled and which they administer, directly or indirectly. It is, of course, possible to expand the national boundaries by penetrating and later annexing adjacent areas, but those who engage in this usually think of it as a manifestation of nationalism rather than of colonialism. Indeed, colonialism now generally means the process by which Westerners gained and kept control of tropical and semi-tropical areas. The original motive may have been to preach or trade or exploit natural resources or gain strategic advantage; if local conditions became unstable, the foreign settlers were tempted to intervene and eventually to establish their own dominance.

Whatever may have been the original motive for the acquisition of colonies (and political motives are usually mixed), most colonial governments came increasingly to manifest some sense of responsibility for the welfare of colonial peoples. What is new in this century is not a sense of international *responsibility* but the principle of international *accountability*. The Covenant of the League of Nations and the Charter of the United Nations have laid stress on the principle that colonial powers are accountable for the discharge of the sacred trust. But whereas the mandates-system of the League of Nations sought to improve the standards of colonial rule, the aim of the United Nations has been to liquidate colonialism entirely.

The elimination of colonialism is sometimes represented as a struggle between pro-colonial and anti-colonial forces, but this is too simple a picture. The truth is that the United Nations has provided an environment which has accelerated a process which was already under way. To the extent that Western colonisers spread democratic ideas in dependent areas, they have themselves promoted the decline of colonialism.

The role of the United Nations in the elimination of colonialism has, in the main, been an indirect one. Of forty-three formerly dependent areas which had been admitted to UN membership between 1945 and the end of 1962, the United Nations played a part in the attainment of independence by Algeria, Cyprus, Indonesia, Morocco, Tunisia, and the former trust-territories in Africa. The UN General Assembly also decided that the former Italian colonies of Libya and Somaliland should become independent within time limits which it established, and made recommendations regarding the formerly mandated territory of Palestine. For the remaining thirty countries, however, the role of the United Nations in the attainment of independence was indirect.

Colonial questions arouse deep passions, and this has obscured the fact that more often than not the issue in the United Nations has been one of pace rather than aim. Colonial powers have contended that it is not in the international interest that power be transferred to indigenous leaders until it is clear that this will not result in a serious decline of material standards or an outbreak of lawlessness or tyranny. Anti-colonialists, on the other hand, have said quite simply that good government is no substitute for self-government. The argument can be pursued endlessly, and in a wider context than that of colonialism. The fact remains, however, that the United Nations cannot be indifferent to threats to world-peace arising either from failure to transfer power or from the inexperience or disunity of leaders who have assumed political responsibility in a former colony.

Colonial territories have benefited to some extent from the arrangements made by the United Nations and the specialised agencies to promote general economic and social development. The United Nations established special programmes of assistance for the former Italian colonies (Libya and Somaliland) and the former Belgian Congo after it became independent. Countries administering colonial territories have contributed more than half of the funds for UN programmes of economic and social development.

The UN Charter outlines the working of an international trusteeship-system for colonial territories on the basis of divided responsibility. *Administration* is by an "authority", designated in a separate agreement for each trust-territory; *supervision* is by the United Nations, acting through the General Assembly and the Trusteeship Council (or, in the case of "strategic" trust-territories, the Security Council). The "administering authority" may be a state or several states or the United Nations itself. In practice, only states have exercised administering responsibilities under the trusteeship system. The states designated as administering authorities are supposed to have complete authority in administrative matters; the Charter sets out various methods by which the United Nations may discharge its supervisory functions.

The trusteeship-system is voluntary; it does not apply to all colonial territories, but only to "such territories . . . as may be placed thereunder". The Charter provides that among the territories which *may* be placed under the trusteeship-system are territories which were detached from enemy states after the first and second world wars. The territories which are or have been under the trusteeship-system are shown in Table VII.

°TABLE VII

TERRITORIES WHICH ARE OR HAVE BEEN UNDER THE UN
TRUSTEESHIP SYSTEM

Territory	Administering authority during trusteeship status	Present status
Cameroons	France	Independent; admitted to UN 1960 as the Republic of Cameroun

Territory	Administering authority during trusteeship status	Present status
Cameroons	United Kingdom	Part united with Nigeria and admitted to UN 1960; part united with the Republic of Cameroun (the former French Cameroons) and admitted to UN 1960
Nauru	Australia, on behalf also of New Zealand and the United Kingdom	Trust territory
New Guinea	Australia	Trust territory
Pacific Islands	United States	"Strategic" trust territory
Ruanda-Urundi	Belgium	Independent; admitted to UN as two states of Rwanda and Burundi 1962
Somaliland	Italy	United with the former British protectorate of Somaliland to form the Republic of Somalia; admitted to UN 1960
Tanganyika	United Kingdom	Independent; admitted to UN 1961
Togoland	France	Independent; admitted to UN 1960 as Republic of Togo
Togoland	United Kingdom	United with the Gold Coast to form Ghana; admitted to UN 1957
Western Samoa	New Zealand	Independent 1962

It will be noticed that Western Samoa and all former trust territories in Africa have now achieved independence, either alone or in association with a neighbouring territory; the territories remaining under trusteeship are in the Pacific area. New Guinea is a large territory with a population exceeding one million, but is still relatively under-developed. The Pacific islands under US trusteeship comprise more than 2,000 islands, of which only ninety-seven are inhabited, spread over an ocean area of some three million square miles; the population is estimated at 78,000 (1961). Nauru is a tiny and isolated island with an area of eight square miles, of which only one square mile is suitable for cultivation; the population numbers about 4,500 (1961). The economy of the island is wholly dependent on phosphate deposits, which are slowly being exhausted.

An administering authority may designate all or part of a trust-territory as a "strategic area". This provision was included in the Charter on the initiative of the United States, and only the United States has taken advantage of it. The Pacific islands, detached from Japan after the second world war, are designated "strategic". The trusteeship-agreement gives the United States slightly more power regarding matters of security than was granted to the administering authorities of other trust territories, and the United States is allowed to limit the degree of UN supervision in areas it may specify as closed for reasons of security.

The Trusteeship Council receives annual reports on conditions in trust territories. When these reports are reviewed by the Council, the colonial powers have tended to be on the defensive, congratulating each other on whatever progress has been achieved during the year under review. The anti-colonial powers have naturally been more critical and probing, drawing attention to deficiencies of administration or to lack of progress in economic and social development. All the same, the Council has been a relatively harmonious body considering the controversial nature of the issues with which it has been confronted.

The Charter authorised two special techniques of supervision by the Trusteeship Council. The first is the periodic despatch of visiting missions to trust territories. These visiting missions have normally consisted of four members, drawn equally from colonial and anti-colonial countries, with a staff from the Secretariat. The United Nations has gained much from the fact that representatives have actually visited trust territories and had direct contact with their peoples and problems. Members of visiting missions from anti-colonial countries have gained a first-hand impression of colonial problems, and the administering authorities have had to be constantly on the alert to discover and remedy grievances before they come to the attention of the United Nations. All the same, UN visiting missions—not being infallible—have sometimes made recommendations which have had to be modified later in the light of other information or experience.

The other special technique of supervision of trust territories provided in the Charter is the receipt and examination of petitions. Several hundred petitions, and possibly thousands of other communications, may be received in the course of a year. It is not always easy to deal with these satisfactorily, since little may be known about many of the petitioners. Some of the petitions have related to matters about which the United Nations can do nothing—for instance, individual matrimonial or financial problems. Petitions have sometimes been couched in very general terms—allegations that the chiefs or officials in some area are terrorising the people. Some petitions have repeated in identical or similar language charges that had been dealt with previously. Some petitions have been vague or unintelligible or anonymous or contained no return address.

All petitions are examined carefully. In the few cases in which petitions are frivolous or deal with matters outside the competence of the United Nations, the Trusteeship Council simply takes note of the petition, or states its inability to reach a conclusion, or perhaps requests further information. In the vast majority of cases, however, the Council is able to draw the attention of the petitioner to some observations of the administering authority or to suggest to the petitioner a form of redress or other course of action. In a few cases, the Council has "invited" the administering authority to take remedial action.

The UN trusteeship-system is, in theory at any rate, less "expert" than was the mandates-system of the League of Nations. The Permanent Mandates Commission of the League was expressly composed of experts who were not official governmental representatives, whereas the Trusteeship Council is composed of states. But any UN organ relies to a great extent on the services of a permanent and skilled Secretariat, and over the years the Trusteeship Council has acquired considerable expertise.

The Trusteeship Council, like the Economic and Social Council, operates "under the authority of the General Assembly". The General Assembly has sometimes allowed political passions to override technical knowledge and has disagreed with conclusions of the Trusteeship Council. By and large the Trusteeship Council has proved to have a better grasp of technical issues than the General Assembly.

It was formerly thought that the close international supervision required by the trusteeship-system would ensure that trust territories would achieve independence more quickly than dependent territories outside the system. Although for reasons of convenience the administering authorities in a number of cases administered trust territories along with neighbouring territories, anti-colonial countries insisted that everything should be done to maintain the separate identity of trust territories until independence was achieved. The Trusteeship Council expressed the view that administrative unions should be strictly administrative in character and should not be allowed to obstruct the separate development of trust territories as distinct entities.

One consequence of this insistence on strict separation has been that some territories have achieved independent status as separate entities when, from an economic point of view at any rate, it would have been to the advantage of the inhabitants to have entered into a federal relationship or complete union with a neighbour. The Cameroun and Togolese Republics, formerly under French administration, have emerged as separate states. In the Cameroons under British administration, plebiscites were held under UN auspices with the result that the northern part joined Nigeria as a separate province and the southern part joined the Republic of Cameroun. In the case of Ruanda-Urundi, formerly under Belgian administration, not only did the trust territory remain separate from the Congo; it achieved independence in 1962 as two states—Rwanda and Burundi.

One form of anti-colonial pressure has been to urge that time-limits or target-dates be established for the attainment of independence or self-government by dependent territories. A stimulus to this came in 1949, when the General Assembly decided that Somaliland under Italian trusteeship would become independent by the end of 1960. Somaliland was relatively underdeveloped; if Somaliland could achieve full independence in a decade, it was asked, why would it take longer for more advanced territories?

In 1955 the Trusteeship Council considered reports by a visiting mission on Ruanda-Urundi and Tanganyika. The mission, by majority vote, suggested that Ruanda-Urundi could achieve self-government in twenty to twenty-five years, and Tanganyika "much earlier". Belgium and the United Kingdom opposed any attempt to fix time-limits for the attainment of independence; the United Kingdom, in particular, maintained that it was impossible to foresee when the essential requirements for true self-government would exist in Tanganyika and that the suggested period was based on erroneous assumptions as to the capacity of the people for development. In the event, Tanganyika attained independence in 1961 and Ruanda-Urundi in 1962.

All territories which had formerly been under the League of Nations mandates-system, with the exception of South West Africa, have either become independent states or have been placed under UN trusteeship. South West Africa was detached from Germany after the first world war and the mandate was awarded to South Africa. In 1946, the South African government stated that a majority of the territory's inhabitants desired its incorporation with South Africa, but the General Assembly would not agree to incorporation. The status of the territory has been in dispute ever since.

South West Africa is, to all intents and purposes, now administered as if it were an integral part of South Africa. The South African government maintains that there is no legal obligation to place South West Africa under trusteeship. The General Assembly, on the other hand, has wished to establish the principle of international accountability for the administration of the territory. The Assembly has insisted that South West Africa continues to have an international status and ought to be placed under trusteeship. It has sought to exert pressure on South Africa by the adoption of resolutions of censure, and by the creation of subsidiary organs for investigation or negotiation. While there have been differences of judgment on legal aspects of the question, the sentiment in the General Assembly has been virtually unanimous in condemning the South African policy of racial discrimination and *apartheid* (separate development).

The International Court of Justice, in response to a request from the Assembly, advised unanimously in 1950 that, while the Charter did not impose a legal obligation on the South African government to place South West Africa under trusteeship, the territory continues to be under the international mandate assumed by South Africa in 1920 and that the South African government continues to have international obligations under the League Covenant. The General Assembly has regarded this as a vindication of its own position and has adopted a number of special rules by which it seeks to exercise supervision over the territory. In 1960 two African members of the United Nations (Ethiopia and Liberia) instituted contentious proceedings against South Africa in the International Court of Justice, and in 1962 the Court decided by the narrow margin of eight votes to seven that it had jurisdiction in the matter. The General Assembly in 1962 reaffirmed its "solemn proclamation of the inalienable right of the people of South West Africa to independence and national sovereignty", and once again condemned South Africa for refusing to comply with UN resolutions. The Secretary-General was asked to appoint a resident UN technical assistance representative for the territory and to "take all necessary steps to establish an effective United Nations presence in South West Africa".

The Charter of the United Nations includes, in addition to the trusteeship-provisions, a special declaration by member-states which "have or assume responsibilities for the administration of territories whose peoples have not yet attained a full measure of self-government". The declaration is explicitly based on two principles: first, that the interests of the inhabitants of non-self-governing territories are paramount; secondly, "the general principle of good neighbourliness, due account being taken of the interests and well-being of the rest of the world". Members administering non-self-governing territories undertake to supply the Secretary-General with certain information; as this part of the Charter has in the past given rise to controversy, I quote it in full.

". . . to transmit regularly to the Secretary-General for information purposes, subject to such limitation as security and constitutional considerations may require, statistical and other information of a technical nature relating to economic, social, and educational conditions in the territories [*other than trust territories*] for which they are respectively responsible."

A declaration of intent to supply the Secretary-General with technical information regarding non-self-governing territories does not seem very far-reaching, but the Secretary-General and his staff had to decide in the early days whether any use should be made of this information. It is, I think, beyond question that UN officials had a clear perception of future trends regarding colonial affairs. They realised that, willy-nilly, the United Nations would be involved in the process of decolonisation, and they believed that it would be in the general interest that UN involvement should be on the basis of knowledge as well as emotion.

The declaration of the Charter regarding the transmission of information has provided the basis for a committee of the General Assembly which "examines" the information. The full name of this body is now the Committee on Information from Non-Self-Governing Territories, but this is usually abbreviated to "Committee on Information". There has been much debate regarding the establishment and work of this Committee; the following questions, in particular, have given rise to discussion.

1. Does the right of the General Assembly to discuss any questions or matters within the scope of the Charter entitle it to examine statistical and other technical information on non-self-governing territories which has been transmitted "for information purposes" to the Secretary-General?

2. Is the General Assembly exceeding its competence in urging administering authorities to transmit information of a political or constitutional nature?

3. Has the administering authority the exclusive responsibility for deciding when security and constitutional considerations justify the withholding of information?

4. Has the General Assembly the right, on the basis of the information transmitted, to make recommendations regarding conditions in non-self-governing territories in general or in a particular territory, and are the administering authorities under an obligation to accept and carry out any such recommendations?

5. What criteria should be used to decide whether the people of a particular territory have or have not attained a full measure of self-government, and should such a decision be taken by the administering authority or by an organ of the United Nations?

These are legal questions behind which has been fought an essentially political struggle. Anti-colonial member-states have wished to establish some form of international supervision over those colonial territories not placed under trusteeship. The response of the colonial powers to this pressure has wavered. Australia, Britain, the Netherlands, New Zealand, and the United States, while by no means enthusiastic, have normally co-operated with the Committee on Information; Denmark also co-operated while Greenland was not fully self-governing. Belgium co-operated in the early days but later declined to take part in the Committee's work. France initially supplied information on sixteen territories, but later decided that the measure of self-government which had been granted to these territories placed them outside the scope of Article 73(e), except for the New Hebrides, which is an Anglo-French condominium. Spain now transmits information on certain territories. Portugal has consistently refused to co-operate in any way.

The administering authorities have been reluctant to go much beyond the strict obligations of the Charter regarding the transmission of information, and have in general held that the Metropolitan Power is in the best position to decide whether a territory enjoys full self-government and thus whether there is an obligation to transmit information. This attitude has not arisen from a desire to withhold information so much as from the fear that the transmission of information may be held to confer on the General Assembly a right to exercise some supervision in the matter. Once information is transmitted, it is likely to be debated; once it is debated, it is likely to give rise to recommendations. Many anti-colonial member-states, on the other hand, would assert that the General Assembly alone is competent to decide whether a particular territory is fully self-governing and thus outside the scope of international supervision.

The Committee on Information has necessarily worked in

an atmosphere of some unreality. It has received very little political and constitutional information, and this is what really interests the anti-colonial powers. Be that as it may, the Committee has done its best to review the information which is placed before it, and there has been a general disposition to make observations in a form palatable to the administering authorities.

As the process of decolonisation has gained momentum, it is inevitable that attention should increasingly be directed to the hard core of territories in which indigenous leaders see little hope of attaining freedom without outside help. The new nations of Asia and Africa have no patience with manifestations of colonialist arrogance. Their problem in the United Nations is to maintain the anti-colonial pressure without going to extremes which would alienate moderate opinion. One of the arguments used in favour of having a special committee to examine information on non-self-governing territories was that colonial affairs could be dealt with more constructively in a small technical committee than in the politically minded General Assembly. Since 1960, however, the work of the Committee on Information has been overshadowed by the activities of the full Assembly and new subsidiary organs. The General Assembly, in December 1960, adopted a declaration on the granting of independence to colonial countries and peoples. Much of the declaration expressed unexceptionable sentiments, and no votes were cast against it. But the inclusion of a paragraph stating without qualification that inadequate preparedness should never serve as a pretext for delaying independence inevitably caused the major colonial powers to abstain on the vote. A year later, the Assembly, having rejected a Soviet proposal for a committee on a *troika* basis to ensure the liquidation of colonialism by the end of 1962, created a Special Committee to examine the implementation of the 1960 declaration.

This Special Committee on decolonisation decided in 1962 that territories in Africa, and also British Guiana, should be given priority consideration. The Committee decided to hear petitioners and receive written petitions. It held more than a hundred meetings in 1962, eighteen of them in Africa, and transmitted to the Assembly a voluminous report which included a review of conditions in the twelve territories which it had considered, as well as detailed recommendations.

The Assembly, on the basis of this report, called upon states administering colonial territories to "cease forthwith all armed action and repressive measures" and urged that immediate steps be taken to enable colonial territories and peoples to accede to independence. The Assembly failed, however, to adopt a proposal to fix time-limits for independence. The Assembly adopted resolutions of a specific character regarding conditions in seven territories in Africa. In connection with the Rhodesias, the Assembly asked U Thant to lend his good offices to promote conciliation among various sections of the population of Southern Rhodesia by initiating prompt discussions with the British government and other parties concerned; but the Assembly did not adopt a draft resolution on Northern Rhodesia which had been recommended by the Special Committee on colonialism. The Assembly asked the Special Committee to continue its work and to apprise the Security Council of any developments in colonial territories which might threaten international peace and security.

UN organs have also intensified pressure regarding Portugal's overseas possessions. The government of Portugal regards her territories overseas as an integral part of Metropolitan Portugal and has therefore refused to transmit information on them to the Secretary-General. The General Assembly in 1960 named the Portuguese territories on which it considered information should be transmitted,* and invited Portugal to participate in the work of the Committee on Information.

During 1961–2, both the Security Council and the General Assembly called upon Portugal to desist from repressive measures in Angola. The Assembly condemned Portugal for refusing to co-operate in the work of the Committee on Information and urged Portugal to transfer power to the people of the overseas territories. In 1962 the Assembly asked the Security Council to take "appropriate measures" (including sanctions in the case of Angola) to secure the compliance of Portugal with its obligations. The Special Committee on colonialism was asked to give high priority to the situation in Portugal's territories overseas.

* See Appendix IX, page 131.

Recent actions of the General Assembly and its subsidiary organs regarding territories not yet independent represent, in effect, an attempt to apply the supervisory methods of the trusteeship-system to territories which have not been placed under trusteeship. Most anti-colonial countries always favoured developments along these lines, but until recently there was not the necessary two-thirds majority in the General Assembly to take important decisions of this character. Colonial powers have always regarded intervention by the United Nations in the administration of colonial territories as contrary to the Charter, and some have been tempted to adopt an attitude of superior detachment to actions of the General Assembly. Experience regarding South West Africa and Portugal's overseas territories, however, shows that boycott or non-co-operation by administering powers does nothing to moderate anti-colonial feelings.

When difficulties arise regarding colonial territories, the normal processes of the United Nations are available. Both the Security Council and the General Assembly have general responsibilities for world-peace; particular functions may be entrusted to the Secretary-General by the policy-making organs; legal questions may be referred to the International Court of Justice. In a recent case, the Secretary-General was given important but temporary responsibilities for the administration of a former colonial territory after a prolonged dispute about sovereignty between Indonesia and the Netherlands.

West Irian (West New Guinea) was part of the Dutch empire in Asia. When Indonesia achieved independence in 1949, it was provided that the future status of West Irian would be determined by negotiations between the Netherlands and Indonesia. Negotiations on the question were held, but without success. Accordingly, Indonesia took the question to the General Assembly. In 1954, 1956–7, and again in 1957, the General Assembly adopted no resolution. In 1955, the Assembly expressed the hope that direct negotiations between the parties would be fruitful.

The failure of Indonesia to rally a two-thirds majority in the Assembly in favour of the unification of West Irian with Indonesia was due in part to the fact that no evidence was presented that such a course was desired by the people of the territory. The people of West Irian, so far as the outside world could judge, were not dissatisfied with the Dutch regime; there was no nationalist movement demanding independence. Indeed, a Dutch proposal to the General Assembly in 1961 that the people of West Irian should exercise self-determination through a UN-supervised plebiscite evoked little support, and the Assembly actually failed to adopt a proposal that "any solution which affects the final destiny of a non-self-governing territory must be based on the principle of self-determination in accordance with the Charter of the United Nations".

An effort to bridge the gulf between Indonesia and the Netherlands was made by U Thant and Ambassador Ellsworth Bunker of the United States. This third-party assistance led in 1962 to an agreement that the administration of West New Guinea (West Irian) would be immediately transferred by the Netherlands to a temporary executive authority under the jurisdiction of the UN Secretary-General. At a later date, administration is to be transferred from the United Nations to Indonesia. After a further interval, but before the end of 1969, the people of the territory will be given the opportunity of determining whether they wish to maintain or sever the links with Indonesia. UN representatives will advise and assist with the arrangements for self-determination.

Much of the work of the United Nations in the colonial field has suffered from the fact that valid points on both sides of the argument have been presented in exaggerated form. Colonial powers would no doubt have accepted criticisms of colonial rule with a better grace if they had been made in a wider context. It can hardly be denied that some colonial territories have been well governed and some sovereign states badly governed, but proposals for comparative regional studies have been resisted by anti-colonial delegates to the United Nations.

Anti-colonialism has been an important and increasingly dominant sentiment since the war, and no state from the Afro-Asian Group has wished to lay itself open to the charge of being "soft" on colonialism. As so often happens, the extremists have tended to set the pace. The more radical anti-colonial countries from Africa and Asia have, moreover, joined forces with the communist states, whose leaders have a well-developed doctrine about the nature of imperialism. The colonial powers have thus been pushed into positions at the other extreme and have been tempted to use political and legal arguments which have been more reactionary than their actual policies.

It is right that the leaders in any self-respecting nation should wish to run their own affairs, and arguments used to explain or justify colonialism which fail to meet this overriding desire cut no ice. The fact that anti-colonialism sometimes takes extreme forms should not obscure what is valid in the doctrine; similarly, the fact that colonialism is sometimes defended in reactionary terms should not obscure legitimate points made by colonial powers. It is undoubtedly true, even though some may think it irrelevant, that some of the more outspoken critics of colonialism represent countries in which there is a notable lack of respect for human rights. The Belgian government, indeed, has held that the Charter provisions regarding dependent areas have been interpreted too narrowly. The phrase "territories whose peoples have not yet attained a full measure of self-government", according to this view, should apply to all non-self-governing peoples, whether they live in colonies or in sovereign states. It is held that the United Nations has been failing in its responsibilities by discriminating between colonialism of the classical type and other forms of subordinate states.

From a strictly legal point of view, much can be said to support the Belgian thesis. All states are tempted to use legal arguments when it suits their interests and to ignore such arguments when it does not. It may well be true that methods which are appropriate for UN action regarding colonial problems of the classical type are not appropriate for UN action regarding the protection of minorities or the prevention of discrimination within sovereign states. It would, however, be a great misfortune were the United Nations to fail to devote to the latter types of problem the enthusiasm and vigour which has characterised its activities regarding the elimination of colonialism.

The United Nations will eventually have to turn its attention to the future of some of the smaller dependent territories. Of nearly eighty territories which are now generally regarded as colonies, some half dozen have populations exceeding one million and can expect to achieve independence and separate UN membership in the 1960s. There are twenty-five or thirty other territories or groups of territories with populations between 100,000 and one million which may also qualify for separate UN membership after independence. Some of the remaining territories may enter into free association or integration with neighbouring areas, but there are about twenty small islands or isolated territories with some kind of dependent or subordinate status having populations less than 100,000 for which no such relationship now seems feasible. Why, as a matter of abstract justice, should these smaller territories be denied the same destiny of independence as larger and more populous territories? Yet how many of them can manage to maintain the full apparatus of sovereignty?

CHAPTER VII

REFUGEES

In the spring of 1958, the British Conservative magazine *Crossbow* carried an article entitled "Wanted: a World Refugee Year". Impressed by the world-wide scientific co-operation in Antarctica during the International Geophysical Year, the authors suggested that the refugee-problem should be tackled by a similar international effort. "With the satellites circling and the tractors chugging through the Antarctic", they wrote, "the International Geophysical Year is producing scientific advances and presumably diverting international rivalry into remoter, less dangerous spheres. On a much smaller outlay a World Refugee Year could yield incomparable dividends in human happiness."

Refugees are the human flotsam left stranded by the tide of war, revolution, or persecution. Even while the second world war was still in progress, the states which later established the United Nations recognised their common interest in and responsibility for dealing with the refugee-problem. When the United Nations Relief and Rehabilitation Administration (UNRRA) was founded in 1943, it was taken for granted that the refugee-problem was an international responsibility.

The United Nations has been mainly concerned with "international" refugees—that is to say, people who have been uprooted from their homeland for political reasons and are now living as foreigners in another country. But there are also many millions of "national" refugees, particularly in divided countries or countries from whom territory has been taken. "National" refugees have also been uprooted from their homes for political reasons but, not being regarded as foreigners where they have settled, do not have the same claim for international assistance and protection as "international" refugees.

Until an "international" refugee is repatriated or finds a permanent home and a new nationality, he is by definition a foreigner wherever he goes. He probably left his own country in haste at a time of political upheaval, leaving family and possessions behind. He is likely to have arrived penniless, and now lives in a makeshift shack or tent or in some dreary encampment. He may be separated from family and friends, perhaps not understanding the language of the country in which he finds himself. He may be old or ill or a child; even if he is capable of work, he may be prevented from doing so by the laws of the country which has given him asylum.

Most refugees need two kinds of help. They need immediate relief in the form of food, clothing, bedding, shelter, and medical care. But they also need long-term assistance and advice about such matters as how they may be united with other displaced members of their family, where they may settle, what sort of work they may do.

Any cross-section of the community will contain a small proportion of criminals, neurotics, misfits, and trouble-makers. Refugees are no exception, but anti-social tendencies cause exceptional havoc in the confined and unnatural conditions in which most refugees find themselves. Refugees do not have the security of a familiar environment. They are unlikely to have the satisfaction of being valued as members of a community. They are usually strangers, waiting to go somewhere else.

Quite apart from humanitarian considerations, there is a reason of self-interest why the international community should seek to ease the plight of these unhappy and uprooted people. If refugees are not decently looked after, treated with dignity and respect, and given a vision of hope, they are liable to become the victims of extremist political forces, of irredentist movements, of racial demagogues.

Estimates of the number of people who have become refugees since the second world war depend on how one defines a refugee. The UN report on World Refugee Year refers to "some 40 million men, women and children" as having become refugees since the second world war, and notes that "perhaps 15 million are still [1960] in that condition". Moreover, there are even some refugees from the turmoils and revolutions of the first world war. And the tragedy is that each year brings new refugee problems—Tibetans, Algerians, Cubans, Balubas, Laotians, Angolans, Rwandese . . .

The *Crossbow* proposal for a great international effort on behalf of refugees was followed up by the British United Nations Association, which set up a special committee to promote the idea in Britain. The British government agreed to sponsor the proposal internationally, and on 5 December 1958 the UN General Assembly formally approved the idea of "a further world-wide effort to help resolve the world refugee problem".

World Refugee Year began on 1 July 1959 and was one of the greatest humanitarian efforts in history. Over $85 million was contributed, two-thirds coming from non-governmental sources. Britain alone raised $25 million, a contribution of 48 cents *per caput*; the *per caput* contribution of Norway was 76 cents, and of New Zealand 52 cents.

World Refugee Year was sponsored by the United Nations, but most international refugee efforts involve co-operation between UN agencies, national governments, and voluntary organisations. The voluntary agencies concerned with refugee problems, of which more than thirty have administered refugee aid programmes, co-operated in an International Committee for World Refugee Year and more recently established a permanent International Council in Geneva to co-ordinate their refugee and related activities. Many of these agencies have consultative status with the UN Economic and Social Council.

The responsibilities of the United Nations for refugees are now exercised through two agencies. One, the United Nations Relief and Works Agency for Palestine Refugees in the Near East, is responsible for more than one million Arab refugees from Palestine who are living in Jordan, the Gaza Strip (administered by the United Arab Republic), Syria, and Lebanon. The other UN agency is the Office of the High Commissioner for Refugees. The agency for Arab refugees is an operational body which carries out direct relief and works projects for a specified group of refugees, in collaboration with local governments. The Office of the High Commissioner, on the other hand, has been primarily a co-ordinating and supervisory body. Both UN agencies seek to work in a humanitarian and non-political spirit; both collaborate with governments and with non-governmental bodies, such as Red Cross and Red Crescent societies and various relief agencies, mostly with religious affiliations; both UN agencies are financed by voluntary contributions, governmental and private.

A special task of the UN High Commissioner has been to secure the maximum international protection for refugees. The aim is to ensure that refugees, until they have either returned to their country of origin of their own free will or have found a permanent home and acquired a new nationality, should enjoy a status as close as possible to that of nationals of the country in which they are living. This is a delicate task since in most countries there is a tendency to give nationals a more favoured status than is given to foreigners. Protection of refugees is secured partly through international legal instruments or agreements (for example, conventions relating to the status of refugees and stateless persons), and partly by national action (for example, removing restrictions on the right of refugees to work or benefit from social security legislation, procedures whereby refugees may apply for naturalisation).

From the point of view of the United Nations, there have tended to be certain features common to refugee-problems wherever they have occurred: the disruptive effect of large concentrations of uprooted people; the fact that many refugees have found asylum first in relatively poor areas where there is a surplus of labour; exploitation of refugee-problems for political purposes; administrative difficulties inherent in co-operation, often on an emergency basis, between international agencies, national governments and private bodies; the question whether refugees should go home, be integrated in the country of first asylum, or be given the opportunity to emigrate somewhere else; the most effective means of preventing indigent local people from masquerading as refugees in order to qualify for assistance; declining morale among refugees as the more energetic are given priority in resettlement-programmes.

It would be impossible, in this chapter, to describe how each group of refugees has come into existence and the efforts made by the international community to deal with them. I intend, instead, to refer to a number of refugee-problems which have aroused special international interest and concern. I should stress, however, that large numbers of refugees have been outside the mandate of UN agencies. In addition to refugees from the Chinese mainland now in Hong Kong and other groups of refugees referred to later, there are Chinese refugees in Macau (a Portuguese settlement) and in various Asian countries. Some two and a half million immigrants from the Chinese mainland who have settled in Taiwan could be regarded as "national" refugees. Among other "national" refugees since the end of the war were the German "expellees" from Eastern Europe, estimated at between seventeen and eighteen million, who settled in East or West Germany; refugees from Eastern Germany who have settled in what is now the Federal Republic of Germany (estimated at about three million) and a smaller number from West Germany who have settled in the German Democratic Republic; between 400,000 and 500,000 Italians, mainly from Venezia Giulia (now incorporated in Yugoslavia) or the former Italian colonies; about 400,000 Finns from Karelia (now incorporated in the Soviet Union); several million Japanese from the former Japanese Empire; several million refugees who crossed from North to South Korea, and a smaller number who crossed in the other direction; several million refugees who crossed from North to South Vietnam, and a smaller number who crossed in the other direction; and several million Hindu refugees from Pakistan in India and Moslem refugees from India in Pakistan, following partition in 1947. These "national" refugees, except for those refugees in South Korea who came within the scope of the UN Korean Reconstruction Agency between 1950 and 1958, have not received direct United Nations assistance, though a few may have benefited from special World Refugee Year projects.

When the second world war ended, the refugee-problem was mainly a European one. There were—and still are—"loyalist" refugees from the Spanish Civil War, mainly in France. Nazi persecution had forced many Jews to leave Germany or German-occupied countries. Political opponents of the Nazis went underground or sought asylum outside the areas of German domination. Large numbers of Poles, Yugoslavs, and Greeks were in Asia, the Middle East, or Africa. The Nazis had been able, by compulsion or bribery, to attract European workers into German war industry. Millions of Germans or

German-speaking people were being expelled from Eastern Europe in accordance with the Potsdam Agreement.

To begin with, most of these European refugees were cared for in camps, pending their repatriation, integration or re-settlement. Which alternative should be open to the refugees became a sharp political issue. The East European governments took the view that displaced persons should return home; those who refused to do so were regarded as traitors who should be denied international protection and assistance. Western governments, on the other hand, had traditionally believed in the right of asylum and held that no refugee should be forced to go home against his will. According to this view, refugees were entitled to humanitarian treatment until their refugee-status ended.

During the immediate post-war period many refugees and displaced persons were settled in Western Europe, the United States, the older Commonwealth countries, or Latin America. Within ten years of the end of the war, the number of displaced persons and refugees in Europe had fallen from about twenty million to 270,000, of whom about 85,000 were still in camps (mainly in Germany and Austria).

The European refugee-population increased with a leap in 1956. Following the Hungarian revolt, 200,000 Hungarians sought asylum in Austria or Yugoslavia, and a fresh international effort had to be made to deal with the refugee-problem. It was one of the ironies of the situation that most Hungarians who were unwilling to go back home were given the opportunity to emigrate to Western countries, taking priority over the much larger number who had been refugees for long periods in Europe or the Middle East. Indeed, the refugee-problem differs from many other problems of international affairs in that the passage of time is not itself a solution. The integration of refugees tends to favour the able-bodied and those with initiative and resources of their own. The refugee-problem thus tends to increase in difficulty as it decreases in size, and this has been especially marked in the programmes of emigration. Countries willing to accept refugees naturally prefer to take the young and the active.

There were, at the beginning of 1962, more than one million refugees presumed to be within the mandate of the High Commissioner. Particular attention was being given to the 57,700 refugees in Austria, France, Germany, Greece, Italy and Turkey (of whom 8,550 were still in camps), 4,200 refugees of European origin on the Chinese Mainland, and 1,850 refugees of European origin in the Middle East and Morocco. It was hoped to close most of the remaining camps in Europe containing refugees within the High Commissioner's mandate during 1962 and to move from China all the refugees of European origin who were able to reach Hong Kong. It was expected that the refugee-problem in Turkey would be entirely eliminated during 1963, and in Greece and Italy by the end of 1964.

Some people become refugees because they leave their homeland, but others are refugees from the day they are born. More than a hundred new Arab refugees are born every single day of the year, and more than one-third of the Arab refugees in the Middle East have been refugees all their lives.

Governments have provided more than $400 million for the care of the Arab refugees since the Palestine war ended. This is a lot of money, although it averages less than 10 cents a day for food, clothing, shelter, health-care, and social services for each refugee. More than 90 per cent of the governmental contribution to the UN agency for Palestinian refugees has come from the United States, Britain and Canada.

It is certainly one of the tragedies of our era that an attempt to solve one refugee-problem helped to create another one. The Jewish people, subjected to ghastly persecution by the Nazis in Europe, dreamed of a haven in what was until 1948 the mandated territory of Palestine. The General Assembly decided in 1947 that the British mandate over Palestine should end in 1948 and that Palestine should be divided into a Jewish state, an Arab state, and an international regime for the city of Jerusalem, the three to be linked in an economic union. This decision was accepted by the Jewish Agency but not by the Arab Higher Committee. Civil war broke out in Palestine, and the Arab exodus began. Following the termination of the mandate, what had been civil war became international war between the newly proclaimed state of Israel and the neighbouring Arab countries, until an armistice agreement was negotiated in 1949 by Dr. Ralph J. Bunche of the UN Secretariat.

When these hostilities ended, nearly one million Palestine

Arabs found themselves outside the borders of the new state of Israel. The Arab countries in which they had taken refuge could not support them without help, and the General Assembly agreed that emergency relief should be sent on an international basis. At first, UN aid was provided through three private agencies: the Red Cross, the Red Crescent and the American Friends Service Committee. Later the United Nations created its own agency for Palestinian refugees.

It is fifteen years since the General Assembly laid down the main principles on which the problem of Palestinian refugees should be tackled. First, refugees wishing to return home and live at peace with their neighbours should be permitted to do so; second, refugees choosing not to return home should receive compensation for loss of property left behind. While there have been technical difficulties about identifying and valuing the property of Arab refugees, the main problem has been essentially political. The Arab states have regarded a satisfactory settlement of the question on the basis of the two alternatives approved by the General Assembly as a precondition of any general settlement with Israel. Israel has been unwilling to allow substantial numbers of Arabs to return except as part of a general settlement of the issues dividing Israel and the Arab countries.

The unfortunate refugees have thus been the victims of a prolonged and bitter political conflict, and little progress has been made towards a settlement. The Arab countries have wanted to discourage approaches to the problem which might seem to imply the permanent settlement of the refugees outside Israel, or any attempts to reach even a partial settlement which do not give the refugees unfettered choice between repatriation and compensation. Israel, for her part, has not wished one million Arabs to return without a significant diminution of Arab hostility. Israel has welcomed a considerable number of Jews from other parts of the Middle East, and it is said that the country could not now easily absorb a large Arab influx.

The UN agency for Palestinian refugees was set up not only to attend to direct relief of suffering, but also to provide useful employment pending a permanent solution of the refugee problem. Relief, if on a minimal basis, has been provided, but the majority of the refugees have been reluctant to co-operate in "works" projects or any efforts at rehabilitation which might seem to affect adversely their desire to return to their homes. A small proportion of the refugees have found useful employment, but the majority have lived in idleness in camps. Even a modest programme of vocational training has had to proceed on the strict understanding that it in no way prejudices what the refugees regard as their political rights.

Various efforts have been made over the years to work out a programme, in accordance with UN principles and decisions, by which the Arab refugees can look forward to a decent future. The most recent official effort in this direction has been made by Mr. Joseph E. Johnson, President of the Carnegie Endowment for International Peace, who was asked by the UN Palestine Conciliation Commission to explore practical means of making progress on the problem. Mr. Johnson visited the area in 1961 and again in 1962, and consulted representatives of the states concerned in New York. Mr. Johnson's proposals had not been made public when this book went to press, but it was believed that they included a plan whereby the refugees would be asked to indicate in confidence whether they wished to return to Israel or accept compensation and final settlement in one of the Arab countries or elsewhere. An agency of the United Nations would extend its good offices in order to help the refugees and the governments concerned to make progress in dealing with the problem. It is clear that the governments directly involved can all point to unpalatable features in a plan of this kind, but there is no hope of ending the tragedy of these uprooted people if all the parties adhere rigidly to negative positions.

Another group of Arab refugees were, in 1962, able to return home in order to start a new life. These were the Algerians, mainly children, women, and old people, of whom nearly 200,000 had fled to Morocco and Tunisia during the Algerian war. The programme of international aid to these refugees was under the joint auspices of the UN High Commissioner and the League of Red Cross and Red Crescent Societies, in co-operation with a number of private agencies.

The former Algerian refugees are almost unique in being able to go home. They have, however, returned to a country devastated by eight years of bitter fighting, their homes destroyed and their land laid waste. But with all the difficulties, the former Algerian refugees have an important asset: hope.

One special group of refugees has been of concern to the United Nations since 1957, though they are apparently not legally within the mandate of the UN High Commissioner. These are the refugees from the Chinese mainland now in Hong Kong, numbering at least one million. The welfare of these refugees has not received sufficient attention, partly because of a number of difficult legal questions.

Governments which support the claim of the nationalist government in Taiwan (Formosa) to be the only legitimate government of China have had to take the legal position that the Chinese from the mainland now in Hong Kong can avail themselves of the protection of the government of China (meaning the government in Taiwan) and are therefore not technically refugees within the mandate of the High Commissioner. The Taiwan government has preferred not to become involved in legal niceties, but has persistently drawn attention to the needs of these refugees. The British government, which exercises sovereignty in Hong Kong, has diplomatic relations with the People's Republic of China in Peking, and the Peking government denies that Chinese refugees need fear persecution if they return home.

The United Nations has not resolved the legal difficulties, but the General Assembly agreed in 1957 that these refugees are of concern to the international community, and the UN High Commissioner was asked to use his good offices to encourage arrangements for contributions in order to alleviate their distress. The British government, while welcoming international assistance, has insisted that relief programmes should be under the ultimate authority of the Hong Kong government on the ground that such efforts, like the colony's own vast programme of social welfare, should not maintain a distinction between refugees and other indigent residents.

The action taken by the General Assembly in 1957 regarding Chinese refugees in Hong Kong has had an interesting sequel. A resolution adopted in 1959 encouraged the High Commissioner to use his "good offices" on behalf of other refugees not technically within his mandate. This decision avoids the necessity of a lengthy legal debate on whether the High Commissioner is competent to concern himself with a particular group of refugees, and permits him to respond to requests for assistance by drawing on an emergency fund. This procedure has been appreciated by several newly independent countries in Asia and Africa which, already burdened with internal problems, found it difficult to cope with the arrival of large bodies of strangers.

"International" refugees outside Europe, for many of whom the High Commissioner has used his "good offices", included during 1962 more than 40,000 Tibetans in India, Bhutan, and Nepal; about 30,000 Laotians in Cambodia; 150,000 Angolans in the Congo (Leopoldville); 150,000 Rwandese in Burundi, the Congo (Leopoldville), Uganda, and Tanganyika; and at least 100,000 Cubans in the United States and in Latin America, and 5,000 Cubans in Spain.

In a world of political instability and change, new refugee problems seem bound to arise. In some cases, neighbouring governments may offer asylum to "international" refugees and be able to care for them without international aid. In the majority of cases, however, the assistance of the United Nations and of voluntary agencies will be needed. There are nearly always political implications of UN involvement, but by and large the United Nations has been able to discharge its refugee responsibilities on a strictly humanitarian basis. But so long as refugee-activities are politically controversial, it seems inevitable that they will have to be financed by voluntary contributions rather than by compulsory levies on UN member-states.* Financing on this basis is an uncertain business.

* The purely administrative expenses of the Office of the High Commissioner are included in the regular UN budget.

CHAPTER VIII

PERSPECTIVE

ALTHOUGH the Charter declares that "sovereign equality" is one of the principles on which the United Nations is based, an outstanding fact about the United Nations system is that member-states assume obligations which may, in certain circumstances, limit their freedom of action. Countries which prefer not to accept such obligations need not join the Organisation.

Moreover, it is not simply that a state knows when joining exactly what the obligations of membership will be, for the obligations can be extended later. If two-thirds of the member-states, including the permanent members of the Security Council, decide to change the Charter in a way that increases the obligations or reduces the privileges of membership, such a change is binding on all, including states which oppose the change. It may not even be possible, in such circumstances, to resign from the United Nations because there are no provisions in the Charter for termination of membership, except expulsion for persistent violations of the principles of the Charter.

It is significant that almost all of the unofficial proposals to amend the Charter envisage some diminution of the sovereignty of states. There have been proposals to reduce or eliminate the right of veto by the great powers in the Security Council, particularly in regard to the peaceful settlement of disputes, to make it obligatory for member-states to comply with decisions of the General Assembly, to increase the functions and powers of the United Nations regarding dependent territories and human rights, to extend the jurisdiction of the International Court in international legal disputes.

This is not to say that the only way to strengthen the United Nations is to extend its functions or increase its powers. Indeed, a reason for anxiety about recent developments has been that the United Nations has had to undertake tasks beyond its resources. One symptom of this is the serious financial difficulties with which the Organisation is confronted.

Moreover, there are segments of opinion in various parts of the world which strongly oppose attempts to transform the United Nations into a world-government, however gradual the process. The Communist member-states have, perhaps, been most explicit about this. The *troika* proposal was, in part at least, directed to this issue. Communist spokesmen do not reject the idea of inter-governmental co-operation, but they have opposed any evolution which would permit the United Nations to take action to the detriment of any group of states. Although the *troika* proposal was unacceptable to the vast majority of member-states, the ideas underlying it have not been abandoned. Soviet spokesmen continue to urge that the Secretariat be constituted on a tripartite basis at all levels, that staff should not be recruited from countries whose "quotas" are already filled, and that no more staff-members should be appointed on a career basis.

The *troika* proposal could not be implemented without amending the Charter, and the Soviet Union and its allies have hitherto opposed all proposals for Charter amendment so long as the Peking government is excluded from the United Nations. This position has even applied to quite limited changes, such as proposals to increase the size of the Security Council and the Economic and Social Council so that the new countries of Africa and Asia could be given larger representation.

One particular question arises whenever Charter review is under consideration. It has been an accepted principle of international affairs that the basic unit is the state. The United Nations is an organisation of states, and each member has one vote. There has, however, been a growing disparity between votes and power since 1945. Two-thirds of the most populous UN member-states (populations exceeding 50 million) were founding members, whereas two-thirds of the least populous member-states (populations less than 10 million) have been admitted since 1945. In other words, there has been a marked tendency since the United Nations was founded for the size of states to decrease, a tendency which is likely to be further accentuated in the future. Moreover, the new states have on the whole less power and fewer resources than the older states. It is theoretically possible for states which together pay less than 3 per cent of the UN budget to outvote in the Assembly states which together pay more than 97 per cent of the budget.

It was sometimes said in the early days of the United Nations that it was absurd that Iceland (population about 200,000) or Luxembourg (population about 300,000) should have the same voting power in the General Assembly as, say, the United States, India, or Brazil. The difficulty, of course, is that the only alternative to equal voting is unequal, or "weighted", voting.

It is not beyond the wit of man to devise a system of "weighting" which would pay regard to such factors as population or economic resources. The budgetary assessments of member-states already take account of such factors. It would be a simple matter to propose increasing the number of votes of states with the largest budgetary assessments, for example, or states with the largest populations, but an amendment along these lines has little chance of being adopted. In any case, it should not be thought that voting is an end in itself. Most major UN decisions depend on agreement, not on numerical voting majorities. The importance of a vote in the General Assembly in favour of a particular measure of disarmament hinges on whether or not the states concerned will comply with it, not on the number of votes in its favour.

There is a further point to be made in this connection. Wisdom is not a monopoly of states with large populations or abundant resources; irresponsibility is not the prerogative of states paying small budgetary assessments. There is no reason to think that to give the most populous or powerful states greater voting strength in UN organs would either reduce the number of difficulties with which the United Nations is asked to deal or increase the capacity of the Organisation to discharge its functions effectively.

The present disparity between votes and power will certainly increase. U Thant has recently suggested that we may expect "a membership of some 126 in the not too distant future", and facilities at UN headquarters are being extended with this in view. Ultimately the membership may well rise to 140 or 150, conceivably even higher, but the majority of the new members will have populations below one million.

As the character of UN membership changes, so the focus of debate and decision changes too. The number of un-committed and neutral states will no doubt increase still further, so that the countries of the Soviet and the Western alliances may find that resolutions on so-called "Cold War issues" increasingly take the form of crying "a plague on both your houses".

As long as there are colonies, there will be anti-colonialism. Indeed, as more and more colonial territories achieve inde-pendence, the greater will be the sense of outrage about those territories that continue to have some form of inferior status.

It is already the case that the United Nations has been much more active in promoting economic and social advance-ment than was envisaged when the Organisation was founded. Yet there is a disappointing aspect to all this activity, because the absolute gap between *per capita* incomes of rich and poor countries has been progressively widening. This gap cannot be narrowed until the less developed countries achieve a sub-stantially higher rate of economic growth than the more advanced areas. The UN Development Decade (a world-wide effort in the 1960's to raise standards of life) envisages a minimum annual expansion of 5 per cent in the economies of the less developed countries by 1970 so that personal living standards can be doubled within twenty-five to thirty years. Affluence can no longer be regarded as the privilege of a few: it must become the goal for all.

Between 300 and 500 million of the world's people do not get enough to eat, and a further 1,000 million live on diets which are deficient in essential elements. Although hunger could be alleviated by the wise use of existing surpluses of some of the developed countries, it cannot be eliminated with-out increasing agricultural efficiency; this is a major aim of the five-year Freedom from Hunger Campaign (1960–1965).

Much suffering could be avoided if only the resources of the earth and the skill of the human brain and hand were used more rationally. The privileged people need not do with less in order that the underprivileged should have the bare necessities of life. Improved methods of agriculture, new sources of energy, electronics, automation, the use of synthetic materials —these are some of the technological advances which can be used to give the people of the less developed areas a reasonable life.

About 8 or 9 per cent of the world's annual output of all goods and services is now used for military purposes, so that even partial disarmament could lead to significant improvements in living standards in both the advanced and the less developed countries.

The United Nations family of agencies helps in promoting economic development in three main ways. The UN Children's Fund (UNICEF) provides food, as well as medical and welfare supplies and services, for mothers and children. The technical assistance programme, in which the United Nations and several of the specialised agencies participate, is concerned with the transmission of skills. This is achieved by sending experts to countries needing them and by providing technical education and training for people from less developed countries. The technical assistance programme is not simply a matter of the rich helping the poor (though the United States has always contributed more than one-third of the budget); the programme is a genuinely co-operative venture. A recent UN study reports:

". . . more than a quarter of the experts serving under the programme came from countries which were themselves receiving technical assistance. Over half of the countries and territories which received expert services also provided one or more of their own experts to serve abroad under the programme. An agricultural extension specialist from Greece served in Iraq; an Iraqi medical *aide* is working in the United Arab Republic; an animal disease specialist from the United Arab Republic is serving in India, an Indian geologist in Brazil, a Brazilian agricultural statistician in Venezuela, a Venezuelan aviation adviser in Ethiopia. Examples of this sort can be extended indefinitely."

The third need of the developing countries is for investment capital. The World Bank and its affiliates make loans, mainly for revenue-producing projects. The UN Special Fund was created to provide grants or long-term, low-interest loans for pre-investment activities such as surveys of resources and the establishment of training institutes; these are strictly outside the scope of the technical assistance programme. The General Assembly has voted in principle to establish in addition a capital development fund, but the implementation of this aspiration depends on the willingness of the economically advanced countries to increase the quantity of their aid or to channel larger amounts through the United Nations. $126 million has been pledged for the expanded programme of technical assistance and the UN Special Fund for 1963, and U Thant has suggested a combined annual target of $300 million by the end of the Development Decade (1970).

Economic and social instability can have international political repercussions. It is instructive to note how many of the political problems with which the United Nations has been confronted could have been eased if not avoided if only economic and social measures had been applied early enough and on a sufficient scale. Governments turn to the United Nations when other methods are likely to fail or have failed, and it is in the nature of things that machinery sometimes creaks. The United Nations should not normally be blamed for international crises, any more than we blame lifeboat-crews for shipwrecks or fire-brigades for arson.

The United Nations often provides a more convenient framework for negotiations than that available through conventional diplomatic channels. Even the great powers may be glad to use UN facilities in this way, as was evident during the Cuba crisis in 1962. Recent negotiations on disarmament have taken place in the UN buildings in Geneva and have been serviced by UN staff. Officials of the United Nations, in such circumstances, play a mainly servicing role, though there may be occasions when an official can facilitate understanding or agreement by behind-the-scenes activities. It is difficult to assess, and impossible to document, the value of initiatives of this kind by officials of the Secretariat; success must usually be anonymous.

There is often an aspect of gamesmanship in international

negotiation. If agreement depends on mutual concessions, it is not surprising that the parties should hold concessions in reserve; the initial position will include elements which can later be abandoned with safety. Negotiation, when it is real, involves a search to discover what there is in the position of the other party which cannot be bargained away. This is inevitably a lengthy process—witness the discussions over the years regarding disarmament and nuclear tests, Germany, Middle Eastern questions or Kashmir.

It is easy to become impatient about long-drawn-out negotiations over such a question as disarmament. If one mistrusts the intentions of one side or the other (or both sides) and therefore believes that negotiations are doomed to failure, or if one believes that disarmament is more likely to be achieved by unilateral initiatives than by international agreements, the spectacle of intermittent but unsuccessful negotiation year after year confirms one's initial scepticism. In any event, there can be circumstances in which unsuccessful negotiation is worse than no negotiation at all. There are, however, two main reasons why the attempt to negotiate a disarmament agreement is not abandoned. The first is that one can never be absolutely certain that the efforts will not ultimately be successful; it is a poor excuse to give up the attempt on the ground that the other side is insincere. The second reason for persisting is that the actual process of negotiation, even if it is inconclusive, can help to increase mutual understanding and reduce tension.

It is noteworthy that in connection with disarmament and other issues which are or have been the subject of negotiation, middle-of-the-road states can play a crucial role when things get difficult. This moderating function is often exercised quietly in the lobbies rather than publicly in the meetings. It would probably have been impossible for all the member-states to have agreed to appoint U Thant as Dag Hammarskjöld's successor had it not been for the unpublicised but persistent efforts of a group of delegates from half a dozen influential even if not powerful countries.

The United Nations belongs to all the members. It is not a panacea but, in the words of Ernest Gross: "a set of rules and a set of tools". The rules are contained in or derived from the

Charter and are binding; the tools must be fashioned and adapted for each job. One tool is to provide a means of discussion and negotiation, whether in public or in private. Another tool is to place an element of the United Nations where a job needs doing. This United Nations "presence" may perhaps be a group of technical assistance experts, or an operation for helping refugees, or a visiting mission of the Trusteeship Council, or an executive authority such as was established in West New Guinea (West Irian), or a UN force of the kind needed in the Middle East and the Congo, or a truce observation unit like that sent to the Kashmir area, or a single diplomat such as the representatives of the Secretary-General sent to or stationed in Jordan and Laos.

There is no knowing where such UN "presences" will be needed in the future or what form they should take. The character of the "presence" established in West New Guinea or the Congo might prove inappropriate if it should be agreed to establish an element of the United Nations in all or part of Berlin. There are, to be sure, general principles on which such operations ought to be based, but the exact form can be determined only when the precise needs are known.

The Secretariat cannot successfully administer peace-keeping operations unless it enjoys the confidence of member-states. The Charter provides that only a man acceptable to the permanent members of the Security Council and to at least two-thirds of the General Assembly can be appointed Secretary-General. The other members of the Secretariat are not appointed by the policy-making organs, but by the Secretary-General himself. This is a responsibility which belongs exclusively to the Secretary-General, so long as he observes the staff regulations established by the General Assembly and recruits staff in accordance with Article 101(3) of the Charter. This Article states that the "paramount consideration" in the employment of staff shall be the necessity of securing the highest standards of efficiency, competence, and integrity, and that "due regard shall be paid to the importance of recruiting staff on as wide a geographical basis as possible".

The Secretaries-General have in the past encountered difficulties in interpreting and implementing these provisions of the Charter. Some states were, in the early days, either unable or unwilling to release persons qualified for work in the UN Secretariat, but considerable progress has been made in recent years in recruiting more staff from Eastern Europe and Africa, particularly for short-term assignments. The proportion of career-staff has decreased from 89 per cent in 1956 to 75 per cent in 1962, and U Thant has suggested that the proportion should remain at about the latter figure. "There are cogent arguments", he reported, "for maintaining the bulk of the Secretariat on a career basis."

The Secretariat needs the qualities of a trapeze artist. Its task is to serve the whole Organisation and all the members, not any sectional interest or ideological viewpoint. The notion of an international interest may sometimes seem an elusive abstraction, but its pursuit cannot ultimately be contrary to the real interests of any state.

The United Nations does not end the need for statesmanship. The United Nations is an instrument at the disposal of states, to be used or misused or ignored. "As long as there are men", Dag Hammarskjöld once said, "they will quarrel; as long as there are nations, they will have conflicts. And whatever theories you have about the deterrent effect of super-weapons, I believe that conflicts may always lead to open strife, an open clash. Under such circumstances and not knowing how far such a clash may lead, I think there is plenty to do for an Organisation like the United Nations."

APPENDIX

I UN MEMBER-STATES (1 January 1963)

member	date of admission	population 1960 (million)	percentage of regular budget 1963
Afghanistan . .	19 November 1946	13·8	·05
Albania . . .	14 December 1955	1·6	·04
Algeria . . .	8 October 1962	11·0	not yet assessed
Argentina . .	24 October 1945	20·0	1·01
Australia . . .	1 November 1945	10·3	1·66
Austria . . .	14 December 1955	7·1	·45
Belgium . . .	27 December 1945	9·2	1·20
Bolivia . . .	14 November 1945	3·5	·04
Brazil . . .	24 October 1945	70·8	1·03
Bulgaria . . .	14 December 1955	7·9	·20
Burma . . .	19 April 1948	20·7	·07
Burundi . . .	18 September 1962	2·2	not yet assessed
Byelorussian SSR .	24 October 1945	8·2	·52
Cambodia . . .	14 December 1955	5·0	·04
Cameroun . . .	20 September 1960	4·1	·04
Canada . . .	9 November 1945	17·8	3·12
Central African Republic	20 September 1960	1·2	·04
Ceylon . . .	14 December 1955	9·9	·09
Chad . . .	20 September 1960	2·6	·04
Chile . . .	24 October 1945	7·3	·26
China . . .	24 October 1945	Mainland 646·5 ⎫ Taiwan 10·6 ⎬	4·57
Colombia . . .	5 November 1945	14·1	·26
Congo (Brazzaville) .	20 September 1960	·9	·04
Congo (Leopoldville) .	20 September 1960	14·1	·07
Costa Rica . .	2 November 1945	1·2	·04
Cuba . . .	24 October 1945	6·8	·22
Cyprus . . .	20 September 1960	·6	·04
Czechoslovakia . .	24 October 1945	13·7	1·17
Dahomey . . .	20 September 1960	1·9	·04
Denmark . . .	24 October 1945	4·6	·58
Dominican Republic .	24 October 1945	3·0	·05
Ecuador . . .	21 December 1945	4·3	·06
El Salvador . . .	24 October 1945	2·5	·04
Ethiopia . . .	13 November 1945	20·0	·05
Federation of Malaya .	17 September 1957	6·9	·13
Finland . . .	14 December 1955	4·4	·37
France . . .	24 October 1945	45·5	5·94
Gabon . . .	20 September 1960	·4	·04
Ghana . . .	8 March 1957	6·7	·09
Greece . . .	25 October 1945	8·3	·23
Guatemala . . .	21 November 1945	3·8	·05

UNEF and Congo arrears 31 December 1962	UN bonds, 31 December 1962		contributions to extra-budgetary programmes, 1961	professional staff in the Secretariat, 1962	
	purchased	balance of pledge		short-term	career
$	$	$	$		
73,688	25,000	—	34,500	—	3
67,772	—	—	4,000	—	—
—	—	—	—	—	—
1,505,748	—	—	60,241	3	14
—	4,000,000	—	1,511,200	2	14
843,847	—	900,000	269,154	2	7
3,035,062	—	—	190,000	1	17
71,723	—	—	—	2	4
429,876	—	100,000	1,197,538	5	10
270,361	—	—	36,765	4	1
—	100,000	—	116,000	4	4
—	—	—	—	—	—
1,552,572	—	—	212,500	2	—
27,298	—	5,000	15,356	—	2
—	9,569	—	8,163	1	—
—	6,240,000	—	7,489,677	6	28
—	—	—	3,811	—	—
—	25,000	—	50,726	3	4
13,813	—	—	8,065	—	—
252,049	—	—	384,762	1	15
9,941,580	500,000	—	60,000	1	46
46,059	—	—	284,729	3	7
25,197	—	—	7,560	—	—
12,558	—	—	—	1	1
31,606	—	—	30,000	—	2
396,599	—	—	70,000	—	5
—	—	26,175	8,960	2	1
3,040,549	—	—	173,610	12	4
7,405	—	—	—	3	—
—	2,500,000	—	2,012,476	—	10
52,354	—	—	—	—	2
34,535	—	12,000	11,129	1	6
21,640	—	—	29,700	—	1
99,450	—	200,000	18,000	2	2
—	340,000	—	61,000	—	1
—	1,480,000	—	200,937	—	5
14,186,015	—	—	4,985,438	10	67
—	—	—	4,102	1	—
16,017	—	100,000	98,352	2	2
297,985	10,000	—	109,000	4	5
48,024	—	—	32,000	1	1

I UN MEMBER-STATES (1 January 1963)

member	date of admission	population 1960 (million)	percentage of regular budget 1963
Guinea . . .	12 December 1958	3·0	·04
Haiti . . .	24 October 1945	3·5	·04
Honduras . . .	17 December 1945	1·9	·04
Hungary . . .	14 December 1955	10·0	·56
Iceland . . .	19 November 1946	·2	·04
India . . .	30 October 1945	429·0	2·03
Indonesia . . .	28 September 1950	92·6	·45
Iran . . .	24 October 1945	20·2	·20
Iraq . . .	21 December 1945	7·1	·09
Ireland . . .	14 December 1955	2·8	·14
Israel . . .	11 May 1949	2·1	·15
Italy . . .	14 December 1955	49·4	2·24
Ivory Coast . . .	20 September 1960	3·2	·04
Jamaica . . .	18 September 1962	1·6	not yet assessed
Japan . . .	18 December 1956	93·2	2·27
Jordan . . .	14 December 1955	1·7	·04
Laos . . .	14 December 1955	1·8	·04
Lebanon . . .	24 October 1945	1·8	·05
Liberia . . .	2 November 1945	1·3	·04
Libya . . .	14 December 1955	1·2	·04
Luxembourg . .	24 October 1945	·3	·05
Madagascar . .	20 September 1960	5·4	·04
Mali . . .	28 September 1960	4·1	·04
Mauritania . . .	27 October 1961	·7	·04
Mexico . . .	7 November 1945	35·0	·74
Mongolia . . .	27 October 1961	·9	·04
Morocco . . .	12 November 1956	11·6	·14
Nepal . . .	14 December 1955	9·4	·04
Netherlands . .	10 December 1945	11·5	1·01
New Zealand . .	24 October 1945	2·4	·41
Nicaragua . . .	24 October 1945	1·5	·04
Niger . . .	20 September 1960	2·9	·04
Nigeria . . .	7 October 1960	35·1	·21
Norway . . .	27 November 1945	3·6	·45
Pakistan . . .	30 September 1947	92·7	·42
Panama . . .	13 November 1945	1·1	·04
Paraguay . . .	24 October 1945	1·8	·04
Peru . . .	31 October 1945	10·9	·10
Philippines . . .	24 October 1945	27·8	·40
Poland . . .	24 October 1945	29·7	1·28
Portugal . . .	14 December 1955	8·9	·16
Rumania . . .	14 December 1955	18·4	·32

UNEF and Congo arrears 31 December 1962	UN bonds, 31 December 1962 purchased	balance of pledge	contributions to extra-budgetary programmes, 1961	professional staff in the Secretariat, 1962 short-term	career
$	$	$	$		
41,883	—	—	5,000	—	—
38,447	—	—	—	—	3
32,385	—	—	20,000	1	1
1,137,198	—	—	108,744	3	2
—	80,000	—	21,074	—	1
—	—	2,000,000	3,150,789	17	42
—	200,000	—	175,000	5	4
102,944	—	500,000	356,000	—	7
152,342	—	100,000	118,058	—	3
—	300,000	—	39,730	3	3
—	200,000	—	118,334	1	3
—	8,960,000	—	80,000	6	20
—	60,000	—	—	—	—
—	—	—	8,385	3	2
—	—	5,000,000	1,982,483	13	12
67,772	25,000	—	141,077	1	5
21,333	—	—	41,000	—	1
31,953	8,271	—	100,452	1	6
—	—	200,000	54,000	1	1
34,108	—	—	54,500	1	—
7,949	100,000	—	17,000	—	2
17,330	—	—	5,102	2	—
14,336	—	—	5,000	1	—
—	—	4,082	—	—	—
1,129,359	—	—	655,293	4	5
—	—	—	—	1	—
147,274	280,000	—	107,729	1	1
50,323	—	—	2,000	1	3
—	687,000	1,333,000	4,452,209	2	21
—	500,000	500,000	798,000	3	5
27,676	—	—	16,428	—	1
20,369	—	—	—	—	—
—	1,000,000	—	—	4	3
—	1,800,000	—	1,457,796	1	14
—	—	500,000	287,553	3	9
52,218	—	25,000	10,000	—	2
54,323	—	—	10,000	1	3
158,745	—	—	169,591	—	4
47,329	—	750,000	191,000	2	6
3,121,919	—	—	285,000	9	17
161,919	—	—	1,000	—	1
1,132,411	—	—	58,334	1	—

I UN MEMBER-STATES (1 January 1963)

member	date of admission	population 1960 (million)	percentage of regular budget 1963
Rwanda . . .	18 September 1962	2·7	not yet assessed
Saudi Arabia . .	24 October 1945	6·0	·07
Senegal . . .	28 September 1960	3·0	·05
Sierra Leone . .	27 September 1961	2·4	·04
Somalia . . .	20 September 1960	2·0	·04
South Africa . .	7 November 1945	15·8	·53
Spain . . .	14 December 1955	30·1	·86
Sudan . . .	12 November 1956	11·8	·07
Sweden . . .	19 November 1946	7·5	1·30
Syria . . .	*24 October 1945	4·6	·05
Tanganyika . . .	14 December 1961	9·2	·04
Thailand . . .	16 December 1946	26·3	·16
Togo . . .	20 September 1960	1·4	·04
Trinidad and Tobago .	18 September 1962	·8	not yet assessed
Tunisia . . .	12 November 1956	4·2	·05
Turkey . . .	24 October 1945	27·6	·40
Uganda . . .	25 October 1962	6·7	not yet assessed
Ukrainian SSR . .	24 October 1945	43·1	1·98
USSR . . .	24 October 1945	214·4	14·97
UAR (Egypt) . .	24 October 1945	25·9	·25
United Kingdom . .	24 October 1945	52·7	7·58
United States . .	24 October 1945	180·7	32·02
Upper Volta . .	20 September 1960	4·4	·04
Uruguay . . .	18 December 1945	2·8	·11
Venezuela . . .	15 November 1945	7·5	·52
Yemen . . .	30 September 1947	5·0	·04
Yugoslavia . . .	24 October 1945	18·6	·38

* In February 1958, Syria and Egypt joined to form the United Arab Republic; in October 1961, Syria resumed separate membership

Sources. Population figures are based on information contained in Table I of the *Demographic Yearbook 1961* issued by the Statistical Office of the United Nations.

Percentage of regular UN budget 1963 from General Assembly resolutions 1691 (XVI) and 1870 (XVII).

UNEF and Congo arrears as at 31 December 1962 are given in ST/ADM/SER.B/168.

United Nations Bonds (purchases and pledges) based on information in Annex 11 of A/C.5/963.

Extra-budgetary contributions from A/AC.96/163, schedules 3 and 7;

UNEF and Congo arrears 31 December 1962	UN bonds, 31 December 1962 purchased	balance of pledge	contributions to extra-budgetary programmes, 1961	professional staff in the Secretariat, 1962 short-term	career
$	$	$	$		
—	—	—	—	—	—
107,404	—	—	150,000	—	2
8,965	—	—	40,000	3	—
—	28,000	—	5,881	1	—
7,507	—	—	3,000	1	—
1,249,477	—	—	52,540	1	12
1,638,647	—	—	136,203	2	13
71,118	50,000	—	144,978	6	3
—	5,800,000	—	3,668,514	2	9
31,752	—	—	85,725	—	6
—	—	—	—	—	—
28,405	160,000	—	321,421	2	5
20,369	10,000	—	—	2	1
—	—	—	7,000	—	3
—	485,000	—	24,460	2	1
—	—	100,000	811,555	4	6
—	—	—	2,800	—	1
5,937,421	—	—	500,000	5	—
46,271,050	—	—	3,675,000	72	2
551,767	—	250,000	1,080,812	7	10
2,936,578	12,000,000	—	14,669,136	14	94
—	59,672,840	—	63,895,407	17	231
25,197	—	—	3,061	—	1
95,315	—	—	—	1	4
302,916	—	300,000	276,500	2	2
67,772	—	—	—	—	—
299,358	—	200,000	570,000	5	5

A/5214, table 27; E/3591/Rev. 1, Annex 1; E/TAC/REP/210; SF/L.39/Rev. 11.
Staff in the Secretariat from A/C.5/938 and A/C.5/933; figures are for professional staff (posts P-1 and above), excluding posts with special language requirements, as of 31 August 1962.

Note. The United Arab Republic's arrears for UNEF and the Congo for the period 1 January 1962 to 30 June 1962 have not yet been allocated between Syria and the United Arab Republic. The contribution of the United Arab Republic to extra-budgetary programmes for 1961 includes sums from Syria and the Gaza authorities.

II PARTIES TO THE STATUTE OF THE INTERNATIONAL COURT OF JUSTICE BUT
NOT MEMBERS OF THE UNITED NATIONS

	population 1960 *(million)*
Liechtenstein	·02
San Marino	·02
Switzerland	5·4

III PENDING APPLICATIONS FOR ADMISSION TO THE UNITED NATIONS

	date of application	*population 1960 (million)*
Democratic People's Republic of Korea (North)	9 February 1949	8·2
Democratic Republic of Vietnam (North)	22 November 1948	15·9
Kuwait	30 June 1961	·2
Republic of Korea (South) . .	29 November 1948	24·7
Vietnam (South) . . .	17 December 1951	14·1

IV TRUST TERRITORIES

	administering authority	*population 1960 (million)*
Nauru . . .	Australia, on behalf also of New Zealand and the United Kingdom	·004
New Guinea . .	Australia	1·4
Pacific Islands . .	United States	·08

V TERRITORY UNDER THE INTERNATIONAL MANDATE ASSUMED BY SOUTH AFRICA IN 1920

population 1960
(million)

South West Africa . . . . . . ·5

VI TERRITORY UNDER THE TEMPORARY EXECUTIVE AUTHORITY OF THE UNITED NATIONS

population 1960
(million)

West New Guinea (West Irian) . . . ·7

VII NON-SELF-GOVERNING TERRITORIES CONCERNING WHICH INFORMATION IS TRANSMITTED UNDER ARTICLE 73(e) OF THE CHARTER

	administering authority	*population 1960 (million)*
Aden	United Kingdom	·9
American Samoa . . .	United States	·02
Bahamas	United Kingdom	·1
Barbados	United Kingdom	·2
Basutoland . . .	United Kingdom	·7
Bechuanaland . . .	United Kingdom	·3
Bermuda	United Kingdom	·04
British Guiana . . .	United Kingdom	·6
British Honduras . .	United Kingdom	·09
Brunei	United Kingdom	·08
Cayman Islands . . .	United Kingdom	·008
Cocos (Keeling) Islands .	Australia	·001
Cook Islands . . .	New Zealand	·02
Falkland Islands . . .	United Kingdom	·002
Fernando Po . . .	Spain	·06
Fiji	United Kingdom	·4
Gambia	United Kingdom	·3
Gibraltar	United Kingdom	·03
Gilbert and Ellice Islands .	United Kingdom	·05
Guam	United States	·07
Hong Kong . . .	United Kingdom	3·0
Ifni	Spain	·05
Kenya	United Kingdom	7·1

	administering authority	population 1960 (million)
Leeward Islands	United Kingdom	
Antigua		·05
Montserrat . . .		·01
St. Kitts-Nevis and Anguilla .		·06
British Virgin Islands . .		·007
Malta	United Kingdom	·3
Mauritius and dependencies .	United Kingdom	·7
New Hebrides	Condominium of France and UK	·06
Niue Island	New Zealand	·005
North Borneo . . .	United Kingdom	·5
Northern Rhodesia . . .	United Kingdom	2·4
Nyasaland	United Kingdom	2·8
Papua	Australia	·5
Pitcairn Island	United Kingdom	—
Río Muni	Spain	·2
St. Helena and dependencies .	United Kingdom	·006
Sarawak	United Kingdom	·7
Seychelles	United Kingdom	·04
Singapore	United Kingdom	1·6
Solomon Islands	United Kingdom	·1
Spanish Sahara (Rio de Oro, & Saguia el Hamra) . . .	Spain	·02
Swaziland	United Kingdom	·3
Tokelau Islands . .	New Zealand	·002
Turks and Caicos Islands .	United Kingdom	·006
US Virgin Islands . .	United States	·03
Windward Islands . .	United Kingdom	
Dominica . . .		·06
Grenada		·09
St. Lucia		·09
St. Vincent . . .		·08
Zanzibar and Pemba . .	United Kingdom	·3

VIII TERRITORIES CONCERNING WHICH INFORMATION WAS FORMERLY TRANSMITTED UNDER ARTICLE 73(e) OF THE CHARTER AND WHICH DO NOT NOW HAVE SEPARATE UN MEMBERSHIP

	information formerly transmitted by	date of cessation of information	present status	population 1960 (million)
Alaska . .	United States	1959	state of the United States	·2
Antilles (Netherlands), Curaçao	Netherlands	1951	self-governing part of the Kingdom of the Netherlands	·2
Comoro Archipelago . .	France	1957	internal autonomy	·2
Greenland .	Denmark	1953	integral part of Danish realm	·03
Guadaloupe .	France	1947	Overseas Department of France	·3
Guiana (French)	France	1947	Overseas Department of France	·03
Hawaii . .	United States	1959	state of the United States	·6
India, French settlements .	France	1948	integral part of India	·3
Martinique .	France	1947	Overseas Department of France	·3
New Caledonia	France	1947	Overseas Territory of France	·08
Oceania, French settlements .	France	1947	Overseas Territory of France	·08
Panama Canal Zone . .	United States	1947	status a subject for study and consultation by the United States and Panama	·04
Puerto Rico .	United States	1953	Commonwealth associated with the United States	2·4
Réunion . .	France	1947	Overseas Department of France	·3

	information formerly transmitted by	date of cessation of information	present status	population 1960 (million)
Saint Pierre and Miquelon .	France	1947	Overseas Territory of France	·005
So m a l i l a n d (French) .	France	1957	internal autonomy	·07
Surinam . .	Netherlands	1951	self-governing part of the Kingdom of the Nether- lands	·3

IX PORTUGUESE TERRITORIES REFERRED TO IN GENERAL ASSEMBLY RESO-
LUTION 1542 (xv)

	population 1960 (million)
Angola, including the enclave of Cabinda . .	4·6
Cape Verde Archipelago	·2
Goa and dependencies: united with India 1961	—
Guinea, called "Portuguese Guinea" . . .	·6
Macau and dependencies	·2
Mozambique	6·5
São João Baptista de Ajudá: united with Dahomey 1961	—
São Tomé and Príncipe, and their dependencies .	·07
Timor and dependencies	·5

APPENDIX

X OTHER COUNTRIES AND TERRITORIES

	population 1960 (million)
Andorra	·008
Bahrain Islands	·1
Bhutan	·7
Bonin Islands	—
Christmas Island	·003
Germany	
German Democratic Republic	16·2
German Federal Republic	53·4
East Berlin	1·1
West Berlin	2·2
Holy See	·001
Maldive Islands	·09
Midway Island	·002
Monaco	·02
Muscat and Oman	·6
Norfolk Island	·001
Qatar	·04
Ryukyu Islands	·9
Sikkim	·2
Southern Rhodesia *	3·1
Spanish North Africa	1·5
Tonga	·06
Trucial Oman	·09
Wake Island	·001
Western Samoa †	·1

* The General Assembly, in resolution 1747 (XI) of 28 June 1962, declared that Southern Rhodesia was a non-self-governing territory.

† Former trust territory, administered by New Zealand; achieved independence in 1962.

SUGGESTIONS FOR FURTHER READING

Bailey, Sydney D. *The General Assembly of the United Nations.* London: Stevens. New York: Praeger. 1960.

Bailey, Sydney D. *The Secretariat of the United Nations.* London: Stevens. New York: Carnegie Endowment for International Peace. 1962.

Bechhoefer, Bernhard G. *Postwar negotiations for arms control.* Washington: Brookings Institution. 1961.

Boyd, Andrew. *United Nations: piety, myth and truth.* Harmondsworth, Middlesex: Penguin. 1962.

Brierly, J. L. *The law of Nations.* Fifth edition. Oxford: Clarendon Press. 1955.

Calvocoressi, Peter. *World order and new states.* London: Chatto and Windus. New York: Praeger. 1962.

Claude, Inis L. "The United Nations and the use of force." *International Conciliation,* No. 532. New York: Carnegie Endowment for International Peace. 1961.

Frye, William R. *A United Nations peace force.* New York: Oceana Publications. London: Stevens. 1957.

Goodrich, Leland, *and* Anne P. Simons. *The United Nations and the Maintenance of International Peace and Security.* Washington: Brookings Institution. 1955.

Goodspeed, Stephen S. *The nature and function of international organization.* New York: Oxford University Press. 1959.

Hadwen, John, and Kaufmann, Johan. *How United Nations decisions are made.* Revised edition. Leyden: Sijthoff. 1962.

Hovet, Thomas. *Bloc Politics in the United Nations.* Cambridge, Mass.: Harvard University Press. London: Oxford University Press. 1960.

Jiménez de Aréchaga, Eduardo. *Voting and the handling of disputes in the Security Council.* New York: Carnegie Endowment for International Peace. 1950.

Larson, Arthur. *When nations disagree: a handbook on peace through law.* Baton Rouge, La.: Louisiana State University Press. 1961.

Lash, Joseph P. *Dag Hammarskjold: custodian of the brushfire peace.* New York: Doubleday. London: Cassell. 1961.

Lie, Trygve. *In the cause of peace.* New York: Macmillan. 1954.

Loveday, A. *Reflections on international administration.* Oxford: Clarendon Press. 1956.

Mangone, Gerald J. *A short history of international organization*. New York, London: McGraw Hill. 1954.

Nicholas, H. G. *The United Nations as a political institution*. Oxford University Press. 1959.

Read, James M. "The United Nations and refugees—changing concepts." *International Conciliation*, No. 537. New York: Carnegie Endowment for International Peace. 1962.

Rees, Elfan. *We strangers and afraid*. New York: Carnegie Endowment for International Peace. 1959.

Russell, Ruth B., assisted by Jeanette E. Muther. *A history of the United Nations Charter*. Washington: Brookings Institution. London: Faber. 1958.

Sady, Emil J. *The United Nations and dependent peoples*. Washington: Brookings Institution. 1956.

Schwebel, Stephen M. *The Secretary-General of the United Nations*. Cambridge, Mass.: Harvard University Press. London: Oxford University Press. 1952.

Young, Wayland. *Strategy for survival*. Harmondsworth, Middlesex: Penguin. 1959.

INDEX

INDEX